Behaviour Skills For Parents, Teachers and Support People

A Parents, Teachers and Support Workers guide to understanding behaviour, and knowing the basics of how to manage and modify unwanted behaviour

Written by Trevor Lewis
BA (Psych) PGDipSci (Psych)

Photo credits: Front Cover– Di and *Katherine Lewis*, Chinese Gardens, Dunedin, New Zealand
Back Cover – Author, Trevor Lewis

Version Two   Copyright 2011   Trevor Lewis   Dunedin
New Zealand

ISBN : 0473180413

FORWARD

By Trevor Lewis BA(Psych) PGDipSci(Psych)
Behaviour Specialist

Welcome to the second edition of my popular book, 'Behaviour Skills for Parents, Teachers and Support People'. I have updated and extended some of the original chapters, as well as adding three extra chapters, Solving Sleeping Problems With Children, Managing Teenage Behaviour, and Preventing the Pain. I hope you will find this book even more helpful than the first edition, and will recommend it to others who need understandable and reliable guidance around behaviour modification.

Behaviour is possibly one of the least well understood phenomena that affects all living creatures on a daily basis. Yet, so many people claim to have special knowledge about it and advise others with little thought to possible consequences that may result from their often ill informed advice.

Every purposeful interaction with the environment around us is a behaviour. Taking this into account, the vast majority of behaviours emitted by us all are appropriate or wanted. That is, the behaviours have a purpose, they cause no harm to us or others and they are understood by those we are communicating with. However, some people's behaviours are harmful to either them, others, or bring unwanted attention or negative comments. In some instances the person emitting them is stigmatised sometimes for life by those very behaviours.

This book is intended to help people who find themself supporting another person who emits behaviour that is unwanted, or supporting a person who needs to learn some new appropriate behaviours. It has been written in a way that will both educate the reader about this important topic, and also help them understand some of the terms and methods used by true behaviour specialists. When I say "true behaviour specialists" I purposely differentiate between those who claim to have expert knowledge, and those who have studied the science of behaviour and have built up their knowledge via experience in designing management plans for people with truly challenging behaviour.

So what is different about this book from the many others out there? Firstly, the author of this book has had several years experience working as a behaviour specialist and has come across some of the most challenging issues possible, from people of average (or above) intelligence and those who were intellectually disabled, had autism, aspergers, fetal alcohol syndrome or other disability. This experience is backed up by several years study (and a degree) in psychology, and two years Post Graduate study (and a PG Diploma) in Applied Behaviour Analysis (the true 'science of behaviour') and Forensic Psychiatry, and has experience teaching others about the skills needed to support people in very challenging situations. This combination of experience and education has given the author a good grounding in understanding the workings of how a behaviour becomes inset, and how it can be modified.

Thousands of people have purchased my booklets on Toilet Training, Anger Management, and Sleeping Issues, and have fed back to me that they have found them extremely helpful, and often commented that the booklets contained information that finally (sometimes after years of seeking help) gave them the guidance they truly sought and they at last saw progress made. I have brought those booklets together into this book, as well as adding an extensive resource around the basics of behaviour modification, some information on crisis prevention, safety and disabilities. My main goal for this book is to help the many thousands of parents, support workers, teachers, and others that desperately seek help that is understandable and workable. I have written it in a way that the majority of people who read it will be able to understand and apply the information presented. It can be read cover to cover for a solid grounding in understanding behaviour (which I recommend), or can be used as an easy reference guide for issues that may be faced day to day, by using the comprehensive index.

Though this book is not a complete resource that contains everything that is to be said about behaviour (in fact, such a resource could take up a thousand pages and still not completely cover the subject), it does contain enough information to actually make a difference to most. Reading and applying the information in this book will help you help others with behaviours that may be impacting on their quality of life, or the quality of other people's lives. At the very least, it will help you to understand the specialists that may come into your life to offer assistance, and enable you to question them if you feel the approach they are taking does not line up with your now well grounded understanding of behaviour.

You will find at times in this book I refer to something called the *'Dior Method'*, this refers to strategies that I have written specifically with the principles of ABA in mind, and also elements of behavioural approaches that I have found successful in my work as a behaviour specialist. The name *'Dior'* is a term constructed from the last two letters of my first name and the first two letters of my Wife's name (Dianne), it is also the middle name of my youngest daughter Katherine. At times in the book you will also find I refer to 'child', but you can also apply these strategies to adults with disabilities, or in fact anyone of any age.

I hope you will find the information helpful, and that you will recommend this book to others who face the same challenges that you do in either your work or family life. In particular I hope that those people who support people with disabilities or support children will find the information useful and relevant to them.

Lastly a special thank you to my Wife Di, and my children Richard, Emma, Samuel and Katherine for their support as I wrote this second edition of my book.

Trevor Lewis **BA (Psych), PGDipSci (Psych**

About This Book

This book is divided into chapters that describe the basics of behaviour management, modification, and important issues that relate to supporting a person who emits unwanted behaviour. There is an index at the back of the book where you can find specific topics that you may want to read up about or refer back to, without having to search through the book trying to find them.

If you want a thorough grounding in the basics of behaviour, what it is, how to change behaviours, how to modify or manage them, then I recommend you read from cover to cover. However, if you just want some quick information on a specific topic, particularly if you are struggling to understand why a child or adult does what they do or having difficulty understanding a behaviour specialist, I recommend reading from the beginning page to the end of the chapter on 'Basic Considerations of Behaviour'. From there, you can then read up more on the topics that you feel you need further advice about by consulting the index.

There are four chapters that refer to *'The Dior Method'*. Those chapters are Toilet Training, Anger Management, Solving Sleeping Problems and Behaviour Analysis. These four chapters can be read by themselves, and give the reader a good grounding in that particular subject, without the need to thoroughly read the rest of the book.

You will also find chapters on Autism, Intellectual Disability and Fetal Alcohol Spectrum Disorder. These chapters contain short informational summaries about these three disabilities. These were included as they are the most common disabilities relating to sometimes unwanted behaviours, and also disabilities that Parents, teachers and support people often struggle to fully understand the implications of, and how best to support the person affected.

The chapter titled 'Preventing the Pain' is particularly aimed at first time parents, and parents with young children who find themselves struggling with knowing how best to help shape their child into a happy, polite and confident young person. My fairly short chapter on Managing Teenage Behaviour, should be helpful to the many older Parents, Teachers and others who have really 'hit the wall' when it comes to dealing with far too common teenage behaviour problems. I wrote this chapter in a different style from the others, to be more of a basic reference to managing common teenage behaviour challenges in a positive, yet successful way.

CONTENTS

Behaviour	-10-
The Science of Behaviour	-14-
First Considerations	-18-
Defining Behaviour	-21-
Basic Behavioural Terms	-27-
Functions of Behaviour	-36-
Basic Considerations	-54-
Safety	-59-
Extinction	-67-
Desensitisation	-73-
What is Reinforcement	-79-
Reducing Unwanted Behaviour	-99-
Teaching Wanted Behaviour	-107-
Modeling and Prompting	-119-
Behavioural Momentum	-126-
Response Cost	-128-
Preventing a Crisis	-136-
Intellectual Disability	-143-
Autism	-151-
Fetal Alcohol Spectrum Disorder	-163-
Analyse and Modify Behaviour	-171-
Toilet Training	-190-
Anger Management	-228-
Solving Sleep Problems	-251-
Preventing the Pain	-270-
Managing Teenage Behaviour	-281-
INDEX	-295-

BEHAVIOUR

Behaviour **is any and every purposeful interaction with space.** That is, every purposeful movement or sound is **behaviour** (not seizure activity, twitches, or other involuntary movements).

So, as you read this text, you are emitting a behaviour - that of reading. Your eyes are moving - and so are interacting with the space around them.

Scratching your head? If you are, this is yet another behaviour, as is clicking the mouse button, shuffling in your seat, calling out to your partner, and so on.

You will hear others, on occasion; make comments like *"I don't want to see any behaviour from you today!"*, or, *"I work with people with disability who show behaviours sometimes"*. If these people did not emit any behaviour it would be likely they were either dead or comatose. The reason you need to have a good understanding of behaviour and its definition, and use the correct terminology is to ensure that communication with others who are also dealing with unwanted behaviour is accurate and everyone is talking about the same thing. Your new knowledge will also help others to understand behaviour, and how they need to develop the appropriate skills to manage that behaviour in a safe way.

So what isn't behaviour? Involuntary movements like gagging, sneezing, and having a seizure, are not behaviours as they are not voluntary. In other words, we have no control over the movement or action.

As we will discuss in a later chapter, all behaviours serve a function to the person emitting that behaviour. For example, scratching your head: function = *stopping an itch*. Moving your eyes back and forth while you look at this text: function = *enabling you to read so you can learn*.

Discovering what the function of a behaviour is, is usually one of the most important steps in being able to reduce or stop that behaviour (if it is unwanted) in the future. There are of course behaviours that are wanted, but are not being emitted currently that we need to teach. For example, a baby who still voids (goes to toilet) in her/his nappy needs to learn the behaviour of using the toilet. In fact this skill will comprise of a few different behaviours including removing her/his pants, sitting up on the toilet, and voiding into the toilet.

You will often hear the term *"challenging behaviour"*, which is usually used to refer to unwanted or inappropriate behaviour. Though all of those terms are not necessarily unacceptable, *I believe it is more clear to use the terms 'unwanted behaviour', to refer to a behaviour that needs to be stopped or reduced due to its impact on others or on the person emitting that behaviour, and 'wanted behaviour' for a behaviour that needs to be taught.*

Before we decide on whether a behaviour falls into the unwanted behaviour or wanted behaviour categories, you need to remember that for a behaviour to be chosen for modification it needs to be established why that behaviour is unwanted. That is, who is it who does not want that behaviour to be emitted, and who decided it needs to be modified and why? For example, when a person tugs on other peoples clothing to let them know they need to use the toilet, as they can not speak or sign - is this an unwanted behaviour? It could be argued either way, but the criteria that should be used is:

Does this behaviour cause harm to the person concerned (including does it stigmatise them)?

OR

Does this behaviour cause harm to others?

If the answer is yes to either of these questions, then it is likely that it is an unwanted behaviour that needs to be modified.

For a behaviour to be identified as a **wanted behaviour** the identifying criteria is not so strict. The questions that should be asked can be any of the following:

Is this behaviour needed to increase the person's independence?

Is this behaviour needed to increase their communication ability?

Is this behaviour needed to reduce the chance of that person, or another person, becoming injured?

If the answer is yes to any of these questions, or related questions, then the behaviour would be categorised as a wanted behaviour and so could be selected for teaching to the individual.

THE SCIENCE OF BEHAVIOUR

Behaviourism - the study of behaviour is a science. Old Wives Tales, articles in popular magazines, ill informed advice from well meaning relatives and even many nannies, should not be relied on to modify behaviour/s that are potentially dangerous or life affecting. This BehaviourSkills book is based on scientifically proven techniques, behavioural strategies that have been trialed by its author, and on well researched information. The author of this book is tertiary qualified not only in Psychology but also in Applied Behaviour Analysis (ABA). It is important to take note that their are some critics of A.B.A., but from my experience these are usually people who have not had full training in it, and so have no real understanding of it. The next chapter contains some basic information on ABA that is important for you to read and understand so you can help educate others on its very important role in behaviour modification strategies.

Applied Behaviour Analysis (ABA) is possibly the only true science of behaviour that uses empirically proven and peer reviewed strategies for modifying behaviour, in the next section I detail the definition of ABA, and some basics around its history and its importance for anyone who has a serious interest in learning about behaviour.

ABA - Applied Behaviour Analysis

For well over 30 years ABA has been the leading reputable approach in modifying behaviour in people with developmental disabilities. But it can be and is also used in many other aspects of life with typically developed adults and children.

This book uses the basic principles of ABA, so it is important that you know at least some of the background around it.

Though ABA has been around for over 30 years, Ivar Lovaas's study in 1987 was possibly what really highlighted the amazing results that can be achieved.

In this study Lovass examined results of his ABA based behavioural interventions on three groups of young children who had autism. Results from the Lovaas study indicated that the children receiving intensive 40 hour per week 1:1 behavioural intervention did substantially better than those children only receiving 10 hours per week or less of intervention regardless of the treatment type.

Specifically, 47% of those in the high-intensity treatment group achieved "normal" functioning, defined as scoring within the normal ranges of intellectual functioning on standardized IQ tests, typical school placement in a general education first grade classroom without assistance, and being described as indistinguishable from their peers.

In contrast, just 2% of the low intensity groups (10 hours or less per week) achieved normal cognitive functioning and attended mainstream placements, while 45% required language impaired classes for mildly disabled children, and 53% following treatment were placed in classrooms for children who were autistic / severely intellectually disabled.

This study proved that ABA can achieve results that virtually no other approach can. It is both scientifically grounded and proven, as well as being accepted by most scholars as being the 'Science of Behaviour'.

ABA today is used in many early intervention programmes, and in many behavioural modification centres around the World. Because of its scientific and proven approach, the principles of ABA are used in all sorts of applications from weight loss programmes to business initiatives.

You do need to beware though that many therapists and even counselors claim they are trained in or have a thorough understanding of ABA, when in fact many have done nothing more than go along to a three or four day seminar. Use the knowledge that you will pick up from reading this book to question therapists who you may come across, and see how in depth their understanding really is. Question them about where they received their training and/or qualifications. Also ask them about previous success, or at least how many times they have used ABA strategies in the past.

You may come across critics of ABA who claim it is punishment based and aversive in nature, this is untrue. Though some of the first years of ABA based interventions may at times have used some punishment based techniques, they are now rarely if ever used. The main focus of ABA is using reinforcement to encourage wanted behaviours over unwanted behaviours. You will also find, as I have, that many of the strongest critics of ABA are those who offer alternative (usually scientifically unproven) methods of behaviour change, and are simply threatened by the real possibility when people realize ABA is the most effective behaviour change treatment, they will flock away from these alternative approaches and so send these critics to financial ruin.

Post Graduate courses in ABA are now taught in many Universities around the World, especially so in North America. The University of Auckland in New Zealand also now offers a full Post Graduate programme in ABA for those interested in formalizing and extending their knowledge.

First Considerations

First Considerations to Take Account of Before Taking a Behavioural Approach to Modifying Unwanted Behaviour Shown by a Child or Intellectually Disabled Adult

When a child or intellectually disabled adult is displaying unwanted behaviour, the effects are far reaching. Not only does it cause immediate issues, such as trying to calm the child/adult and redirect them to an appropriate behaviour, but the incident has now set off a domino-like reaction.

Parents, support people, siblings, and sometimes others can be affected by one person's unwanted behaviour. Soon the Parents or caregivers are losing sleep, and/or being physically and mentally worn out from dealing with the person's behaviour. Siblings can also be affected, sometimes copying the behaviours they have seen.

The first approach you must take to provide much needed help to your child / family member and your family, is to look at possible unseen causes for the behaviour. Before we look at strategies to trial in modifying the unwanted behaviour/s, we must suggest the following is first done:

- **Have a full medical check held for the child/adult.** Ensure there is not a medical condition contributing to the unwanted behaviour. Ask your GP for a full check including blood tests to ensure blood sugar levels, etc are normal. Also ask that basic eyesight and hearing tests be undertaken. If any concerns from any of these tests are expressed, ask that a referral to a pediatrician or other appropriate specialist be made to ensure all biological based avenues are explored, and issues managed appropriately.

- **If a recent dental examination (within the last three months) has not been held, then book your child / family member in for a dental check.** Though we naturally feel that our child or family member would let us know if they had dental discomfort, sometimes this is not the case. They may have dental pain, but not be able to explain the problem, or are frightened of admitting this as they (like many of us) do not like visits to the dentist, and subsequently their discomfort is relayed by their behaviour instead.

- **If school age, check with your child's teacher, and if necessary the school principal that there is no bullying** (verbal or physical) going on. Also, is your child struggling with their work? Is the work load too much, or even too easy (meaning they are bored at school).

- **Are you spending enough time with your child / family member when they are *not* emitting unwanted behaviour??** That is, do they get attention when they are being good, or is behaving in the way they sometimes do, the only way they can get you to attend to them?

GP Check, Dental Exam, School Issues, attention for being good and rule out obvious problems first

DEFINING BEHAVIOUR

You may have heard people in the past talk about the **ABC's of behaviour**, so what exactly does this mean?

In the first few pages of this book I mentioned assessing behaviour, and discovering the function of behaviour as an important first step in planning how to modify that behaviour. To do this, we need to examine each part of that behaviour. Those 'parts' are as follows:

Antecedent

Antecedent simply refers to what happened immediately before the behaviour. Often people place huge emphasis on this, and then try and change things for the person so they never experience that specific event – and subsequently (fingers crossed) do not emit that behaviour again. However, logic would suggest that attempting to shelter someone from certain aspects of everyday life could only result in a lot of extra stress for those supporting that person, and the person never actually learning ways of dealing with the situation. For example, take a child who screams and cries every time they go in the supermarket, as in the past they have received a chocolate or a drink to 'shut them up'. If we were to take the advice of some of the 'experts' we should then avoid going into the supermarket with that child ever again – problem solved. Obviously a ridiculous solution, as the child has learned nothing, and you will one day face a time where they must accompany you into a shop – so what happens then?

It is important though to know what the antecedents are, as this helps you in your analysis of the function of the behaviour, in turn aiding you with a solution in reducing or possibly eliminating the problem.

I suggest antecedents are usually whatever happens immediately (within 30 seconds) before the behaviour is first observed.

There are times however where we need to look back much further to find the antecedents that directly related to the specific incidence of behaviour. For example, if little Joe bumps into his sister at 9am in the morning, with Mum standing nearby – his sister may very well give him a menacing look, yet nothing else. An hour later when Mum is outside talking with the neighbor, sister takes the opportunity to walk up behind little Joe and push him over, grazing his knee. The antecedents we would be interested in knowing are: what happened thirty seconds before the behaviour, and what happened leading up to that period that relates, or may relate, to this behaviour. The answers are 1) Sister ran up behind Joey, while Mum was busy at another task. 2) Joey bumped into Sister an hour beforehand. Remember though that we are talking about the science of behaviour, and so we need to stick to observable facts, not assumptions. We could easily be led to assume that Joe bumping into his sister an hour earlier led to her now pushing him over. Yet, sometime later we may discover his sister had actually been attempting to initiate interactive play (obviously not very appropriately) with Joe, hoping he would, after being pushed over, chase her around the yard giving her some fun to enjoy. So, if the behaviour of concern was Joe's sister pushing Joe over on a regular basis, we would not just need the information about the antecedent on this one occasion, but we would need to look at the antecedents from at least three occasions (preferably more) –so we could see if there was some form of pattern.

Of course we don't want to let the behaviour continue occurring when our intervention could prevent Joe from getting pushed over and hurt, but if the incidents do occur despite our best attempts to monitor and intervene, we would certainly want to start recording some data so to be in a better position to devise a strategy which will in turn reduce or eliminate the behaviour of concern.

To summarise, antecedents are the things that happen immediately before the behaviour of concern. However, we suggest you take into account specifically the events within 30 seconds before the behaviour was observed, **and** review other events that are likely to be related to the behaviour within the last 12 hours. It is rare to find events that have happened long before the 12 hours that are directly related to the behaviour of concern, though this is not impossible.

Behaviour

Yes, we are looking at the 'parts' that make up a behaviour, but this second 'part' we also refer to as behaviour, as it is what actually took place after the antecedent.

The behaviour is what was observed to actually happen. What did you see, hear, and sometimes - feel? Did they throw the remote control from their right hand or their left? Did they throw it at a person, or at the wall? Was it with force, or soft? You need as much detail to the behaviour itself as possible. In my years of work in the disability sector too often I have read incident forms or been told descriptions such as *"Jo was aggressive to me"* or *"He destroyed the plant"*. It is not helpful in making recordings of behaviour to later assess if there is not a clear description of exactly what happened. Having a description like *"Jo hit me once with his right hand, in a closed fist, with enough force to cause redness to my cheek. As he did this he shouted 'too loud noise"*, obviously is a lot more descriptive, and so helpful to your analysis, than *"Joe was aggressive to me"*.

Consequence

What happens immediately after the behaviour has occurred is the consequence to that behaviour, and also - more importantly – determines the likelihood of that behaviour being repeated in the future. If the events that occur in response to the behaviour do not occur immediately after the behaviour, they are not consequences – or at least not in the science of behaviour. So, all those parents out their who use that all too common comment *"Wait until your Mother/Father gets home"*, have wasted their breath. The chances of what Mother or Father does when they get home actually having an effect on that behaviour being repeated in the future or not, are very slim. In the chapter on reinforcement, we discuss how you can link a behaviour with a reinforcer (consequence) that occurs later (or a delayed reinforcer) by using 'bridging reinforcers'.

Consequences are sometimes referred to as reinforcers (or punishers) in ABA, and so this is the terminology we will usually use as you continue through the rest this book.

Reinforcers can be positive or negative, and there are also punishers. Positive reinforcers are **things that happen** to the person emitting the behaviour, or **items given** to the person, immediately after the behaviour occurs that increase the likelihood of that behaviour being repeated in the future. For example, a young infant takes her first few steps, the parent runs to her, hugs her, smiles, and says *"Well done, that's fantastic, great job!"* These are positive reinforcers, and will encourage the child to repeat the behaviour (walking) again. Negative reinforcers also encourage the behaviour to be repeated. Contrary to popular belief, negative reinforcers are not punishers. A negative reinforcer is something that is removed that encourages the person to repeat the behaviour. For example, let's say a worker is under extra supervision because of their poor work performance. As their work improves, the Supervisor spends less and less time watching them work. This is removing the level of supervision (a negative reinforcer) and so encourages the worker to continue his good work in the future so he doesn't have his Boss staring over his shoulder any more.

These three - ABC's - of behaviour are very important to understand and remember. One aspect of the ABC's often not fully understood, is that of reinforcement (or consequence in the ABC). Some people confuse bribery with reinforcement, and so are reluctant to follow advice around reinforcing wanted or appropriate behaviours. Bribery differs from true reinforcement in that it is often presented before the wanted behaviour is emitted. That is, the support person gives the person something in the hope that they will do what is asked of them afterwards, for example: *"Here is five dollars Jim, now since I have given you this I expect you to get dressed in time for the outing today."* Of course, Jim may or may not get dressed in time, because he has already received the item he wanted, so what does it matter whether he does or doesn't do what he is asked later?

A reinforcer always occurs after and only if the wanted behaviour has been emitted.

BASIC BEHAVIOURAL TERMS

This chapter presents the more common terms used by behaviourists, and many of the terms discussed in this book. To be able to discuss behaviour with specialists, or co-workers/family members who have also studied the science of behaviour, you will need to know these terms.

Target Behaviour: The behaviour that is the focus of the assessment or strategy being trialed. It is important to carefully define and describe which behaviour is being targeted for modification and the parts of that behaviour so changes can be measured.

Emit: The verb emit is used in conjunction with the term *behaviour* as it puts emphasis on the fact that reinforcement of the behaviour is what determines the likelihood of that behaviour being repeated again in the future. This is in difference to stressing the antecedent is the controlling factor in the behaviour occurring again, which it is not.

Applied Behaviour Analysis: The scientific study of behaviour. Also known as ABA, this field of study far outweighs any of the other so-called therapeutic approaches to behaviour management and modification in its scientific backing.

"The term 'behavior analysis' was coined by B. F. Skinner, generally considered the founder of behavior analysis. The term was meant to distinguish the field as one that focuses on behavior

as a subject in its own right, rather than as an index or manifestation of something happening at some other level (in the mind, brain, psyche, etc.).

Skinner believed that thinking and feeling were covert forms of behavior. "Thoughts and feelings do not explain behavior," he wrote, "they are more behavior to be explained."

Skinner thought that the concept of mind belonged to the philosophers, and that science should focus on behavior. These ideas form the core of behavior analysis today." (Association for Behaviour Analysis International).

Applied: ABA includes the term 'applied' to refer to the behaviour under study being a socially significant behaviour to the person being assisted. That is, the behaviour that we want to change should be of importance to the individual in their daily life. Such behaviours as learning how to speak, read, and not harm themself are some examples of thousands of possibilities.

Behavioural: For the science of behaviour, to be kept just that - a science, some principles of behaviour must be adhered to. Firstly, there must be a need to actually change the behaviour being changed. That is, we do not just go about changing a behaviour because we decided we didn't like it! The behaviour must be measurable, and subsequently must be able to be observed. We will not know whether we have changed a behaviour or not if it can not be observed and measured. Lastly, we must know whose behaviour it is that has changed. That is, has the subject's behaviour actually decreased from our strategy or is it our behaviour of observation that has changed and so recorded a lower frequency of the behaviour? We need to guard against bias in our monitoring of any behaviour changes. That is, ensure we don't see what we want to see, rather than what actually is being observed.

Analytic: To be analytic when we use our behaviour skills, we must be able to show that the strategy we are using to reduce (or increase) the selected behaviour, actually is the reason behind the change in that behaviour. To do this, we should be able to show we have some control over when the behaviour occurs and when it doesn't (or at least how our strategy or intervention can lessen the behaviour). This is often termed a functional relationship, between the intervention and the behaviour.

Reinforcer: A **positive reinforcer** is something that the subject wants to receive that is paired with the behaviour we want to increase. That is, the person receives something for emitting the wanted behaviour. For example, a child cleans his room, and in return he receives an extra 20 minutes on the playstation. A young man who screams continuously at his vocational setting receives a trip in the van when he has **not** screamed for 20 minutes.

A **negative reinforcer** is something that the subject does not like, **that is removed** because they emitted the wanted behaviour. For example, you start your car up and a buzzer sounds until you click your seat-belt, which in turn removes the buzzing sound (it stops once the seatbelt is clicked in). A lock on the toy cupboard is opened (locking is removed), when the child has cleaned their room.

Note: *To be effective, the reinforcer must be given immediately after the behaviour was emitted.*

Punisher: A punisher is an event that takes place immediately after a behaviour is emitted, and is something that the subject does not want to receive. Some examples are: A speeding driver gets pulled over and given a ticket. Two children have the TV turned off because they are fighting.

It is important to note that BehaviourSkills does NOT endorse the use of punishment. In particular, we strongly advise against the use of any form of physical punishment for ethical, legal, and moral reasons. However, punishment based strategies are sometimes used as a last resort when all other behavioural interventions have failed and the behaviour is harmful to the person concerned or those around them. These punishment based strategies should only ever be utilised by professional therapists under close observation and scrutiny of their peers. BehaviourSkills does not teach any punishment based strategies, and takes no responsibility for anyone holding a BehaviourSkills certificate who tries to implement a punishment based strategy.

Antecedent: The event or circumstances immediately before the behaviour was emitted. For example, dog runs up to you, you shout out in fright. The dog running up to you was the antecedent.

Consequence: This is what happens immediately after the behaviour was emitted. As in the above example, a dog runs up to you, you shout out in fright, your friend next to you tells you *"It's ok, the dog doesn't bite"*. The consequence was your friend telling you the dog does not bite.

Response: The same as consequence, but the term more commonly used by applied behaviour analysts instead of consequence.

Modeling: Modeling a behaviour is demonstrating the correct behaviour so the person seeing that behaviour knows how they are expected to act. For example, you use your knife and fork to eat an omelet, so the person taught can see the correct behaviour (rather than just using the knife). Usually you would be using other behavioural strategies to help teach the desired behaviour as well (if required).

Schedule of Reinforcement: Reinforcers are often set to a schedule. For example, an intermittent schedule of reinforcement would see reinforcers only presented occasionally, not every time the wanted behaviour was emitted. E.g. When the person hands over a card with a picture of a toilet, indicating they need the toilet - instead of screaming like they used to, sometimes the teacher says *"Well done, lets go to the toilet"* and pats them on the shoulder, other times the Teacher simply says *"Go to the toilet then"* and guides them there.

Prompt: A prompt is providing a reminder, a hint, a request, some assistance, for the person to perform a wanted behaviour. These prompts can be verbal, e.g. *"Now, pick up the pen and write T for Thomas"*, or physical, e.g. Holding Thomas's hand and guiding it to the pen, then moving the pen in his hand in the shape of a T on the paper. This is usually referred to as a hand-over-hand prompt.

Fading: Fading is the term referred to when we slowly decrease the frequency or intensity of a prompt that we are using to teach a new behaviour. Fading should result in the person becoming less and less reliant on our prompt to perform the wanted behaviour.

Task Analysis: A task analysis involves breaking down a complex skill or a series of behaviours into single achievable and teachable steps. This will also often involve assessing the skill level of the person or population being taught, so the size of the steps to be taught is also known. *See Behaviour Chains below.*

Behaviour Chains: A behaviour chain is a series of responses making up a specific behaviour. This series of responses (or steps) is usually first set from a task analysis being carried out. For example, the task analysis of pouring a glass of milk would look something like this**:**

Locate cupboard with glasses

Select a glass

Place glass bottom down on kitchen bench

Locate fridge

Open fridge

Locate milk bottle

Remove milk bottle from fridge

Remove lid from milk bottle

Pour milk into glass, until almost to the top of the glass

Place lid back on bottle

Place milk back into fridge

Close fridge door

As you can see, there are many steps to performing even a basic behaviour like getting a glass of milk. Depending on the level of understanding you may need to break the steps into even smaller ones, or you may be able to make the steps less detailed and fewer. For example: Get a glass from the cupboard. Get milk bottle and open it. Pour the milk into the glass, until the glass is nearly full. Put lid back on milk bottle.

The benefit of looking at a behaviour chain is it enables you to come up with the steps you may need to teach a person learning a new behaviour. The following two types of behaviour chains demonstrate why you need this knowledge.

Backward Chaining: In backward chaining you teach a behaviour by getting the person to perform the last step first, then the last two steps, and so on until he/she has learned each step and can perform the behaviour by themselves. For example, learning how to tie a shoelace, you do all the steps right up to pulling the bows tight, where you hand-over-hand prompt the person to do this last step. After they have mastered this step, you then get them to pull the second bow through the first bow and then pull tight, and so on. Reinforcement is provided when the last step is performed without a prompt. As each prior step is mastered, the next step (which they have already mastered) acts as a reinforcement itself as the individual is pleased he/she reached that next step which they know will lead to the very last step - where they get the reinforcer.

Forward Chaining: Naturally enough, this is pretty much the opposite of backward chaining. Here you provide a prompt (as needed) to perform the first step, and do the rest of the steps yourself. When the person has mastered the first step without a prompt, you reinforce the behaviour, then only provide a prompt for the next step, and so on. Only provide reinforcement on the last step mastered (Where that step is number one, then two, then three, etc).

Stimuli/Stimulus: We often refer to stimuli or stimulus when discussing problematic behaviour. Stimuli can be anything that brings about a response of some type from someone. They can be sounds (audible stimuli), sights (visual stimuli), smells (olfactory stimuli), touch (tactile stimuli), or even specific tastes.

Baseline: This term is used for the original level (frequency/intensity) of behaviour being emitted before any conditions (Behavioural Strategies) are put in place. Some behavioural Strategies will include a phase where 'back-to-baseline' is sometimes mentioned, this refers to after applying a strategy, a test is then done without the strategy in place to see what level the behaviour is at when the strategy is removed. This helps to show the functional relationship between the strategy and the behaviour (i.e. does the strategy have an effect?).

FUNCTIONS OF BEHAVIOUR

The information covered in this chapter is to give you only a brief overview of functional assessments, and unless you are entirely comfortable with what you are doing, and confident you have all the knowledge required, you would not normally attempt a functional assessment without professional guidance through each step.

This chapter starts with two case studies that will be used to show how you can undertake a basic functional assessment. It is important to note here that a full Functional Assessment and Functional Analysis take a great deal of time, and a fair amount of expertise. We will not go into any depth of explaining how to do these, but instead offer the following information that will at the very least help you understand the importance of this process. It will also allow you to work on day to day less challenging behaviours, and guide you how to approach modifying or managing them.

The name, location, and other details of the people in these case studies have been changed to protect their privacy.

Case Study One: Sarah G. is 35 years old and has a moderate intellectual disability (also known as a learning disorder, or mental retardation). Sarah has been attending art and craft programmes three times each week for the past two years, and normally enjoys them and participates in most parts of the programme.

For the last two weeks though, Sarah has begun screaming for prolonged periods of time, and the support staff have great difficulty trying to comfort her, or redirect her to more appropriate behaviour. Though Sarah has reasonable verbal communication skills, she can not give an exact answer to why she screams.

Case Study Two: Ben R. is 5 years old, and has autism. He can speak fairly well - though not to the same ability as his peers, and appears to understand around 75% of spoken language from his parents and teachers.

Ben R. wakes up each night at 3am, and starts playing noisily with his toys - staying awake right through until it is time for school, and has been doing this for the last 12 months. Despite not going to bed until 10pm, and his parents trying to redirect him back to bed and sleep, he continues with this sleeping pattern.

In both these case studies, it is obvious that the behaviours are socially significant (that is, they are impacting negatively on others in the environment). In the case of Sarah, her support staff and her peers are already becoming unsettled and annoyed by her screaming. Ben's behaviour is causing the Parents and his brother to be woken most nights, and kept awake - everyone is losing valuable sleep.

The first step in assessing the function of an unwanted behaviour, is defining exactly what the behaviour is. That is, what happens - what does the person do, and say? Break this down into a description clear enough that anyone else can observe when this behaviour occurs compared to what may be another very similar behaviour occurring. We can not measure a behaviour or even try and determine its function if we do not know precisely what the target behaviour is (and is not). For example *"Charlie hits others"* is too abstract to be able to even think about working on a solution. *"Charlie hits other children only inside his classroom by using his right hand, formed into a fist, making contact with others with enough force to cause pain, usually hitting them in the stomach"*, this is a more concrete definition of the target behaviour.

Next we need to determine how long the target behaviour has been occurring, and whether the behaviour is socially significant. That is, does it actually need to be changed; if it isn't causing anyone any harm, why should the person not do it? We can see that in these two studies the length of time is already established, as is the need for the behaviour to change.

We then need to know the following:

When did the behaviour first occur?

How long does it last each time it occurs?

*Where does the behaviour occur?

*What times and/or days does it occur, and how often?

*Who is usually present when the behaviour occurs?

What exactly happens when the person emits that behaviour (That is, what do they do, say, etc?)

How long does the behaviour last?

What happens before the behaviour occurs?

*What happens in the environment when the behaviour is occurring?

*What happens immediately after the behaviour?

Also look at the opposite of the questions with an asterisk. That is, where doesn't the behaviour occur? What times and/or days doesn't it occur? Who isn't usually present when the behaviour occurs? What isn't usually happening when the behaviour is occurring? What doesn't happen immediately after the behaviour? Some of these will make more sense when you read the next page of this chapter that shows mock-up notes of the assessment in the first case study (Sarah). Before you go to the next page, again read the description given about Sarah at the top of this page.

To get the answers to these questions, and for them to have some value, as many people as possible need to be asked for this information (either as a group, or possibly better still - individually so as not to allow members of the group to be biased by other members answers). Of course, if you are a parent or the sole support person, you can actually go through these questions yourself - it will be helpful to write them down if you are to then work out (unbiased) what the function of the target behaviour may be.

In many cases, if the person isn't someone you are close too already and regularly see the target behaviour yourself (such as the parent, family member, key support person, or teacher) you may need to observe the person yourself if you are to do a basic functional assessment and come up with a behavioural strategy for reducing or eliminating the behaviour.

Case Study One: Sarah. *Unwanted Behaviour = screaming*

Definition of target behaviour

Sarah lets out a high to medium pitch scream, with some sobbing also occurring as part of the scream. At times the scream is interrupted by a shout of the words *"I want to go home"*. Scream lasts for around 4-6 seconds, then stops for up to 10 seconds before reoccurring.

When did the behaviour first occur?

Three weeks ago, on a Monday morning.

How long does it last each time it occurs?

Usually around 5 minutes

*Where does (doesn't) the behaviour occur?

Almost always when Sarah is inside the main building, staff can not remember when/if it has happened outside of the art + craft facility. There are only three reports of the screaming occurring in the home environment. There are no reports of the behaviour occurring in an outside environment.

*What times and/or days does it (doesn't it) occur, and how often?

Can occur most times through the day, but more so in the mornings and leading up to meal times (tea breaks and lunch). There are no reports of the behaviour occurring after 6.30pm.

*Who is (isn't) usually present when the behaviour occurs?

Can be anyone, but rarely happens when the Manager is present in the building. The behaviour has never occurred when staff member Mary is working in the same environment as Sarah.

What exactly happens when the person emits that behaviour (That is, what do they do, say, etc?)

Starts screaming - non specific high to medium pitch sound, high volume. Sometimes shouts *"Want to go home"* as part of the behaviour.

How long does the behaviour last?

Usually off and on every 2 - 4 hours (each scream lasting 4 to 6 seconds, with only 10 seconds between screams). Each episode of screams lasts around five minutes in duration.

What happens before the behaviour occurs?

Can be anything, but more often as meal time preparations occur, and when others are eating.

*What happens (doesn't happen) in the environment when the behaviour is occurring?

Other people often become upset at the noise, sometimes shout at Sarah to stop, to *"Shut up",* or they move away from her. No one attempts to move everyone away from Sarah.

*What happens (doesn't happen) immediately after the behaviour?

Sometimes staff and other people with disabilities talk about how annoying the behaviour is, and how they hope she doesn't do it again. No one approaches Sarah when screaming has stopped.

As mentioned in the opening paragraphs of this page, you may also need to observe the person yourself, if you do not already know them and/or have not seen the target behaviour before. Using an ABC chart is one of the best ways of recording down information from your (and/or others) observations. An example of an ABC recording chart is shown below.

EXAMPLE OF AN ABC RECORDING CHART

Name of Person Observed:	Observation Date:
Observer:	Time:
Environment:	People Present:
Target Behaviour:	

ANTECEDENT	*BehaviourSkills* BEHAVIOUR	CONSEQUENCE

If the information available from questioning others does not provide adequate material to come to any hypothesis, and you decide to do some observations yourself, it would also be beneficial to engage one or two others to also do some observations and fill in an ABC recording form. You can then compare your data, and possibly come to some hypotheses about the function of the target behaviour quicker and easier.

However, observing behaviour and recording data is not quite as easy as it sounds - it is important to have consistency and reliability in the data collected.

Basics of Observing Behaviour

All changes to the environment will almost always have an impact, even if small, on a person's behaviour. It is for this reason that your observations need to be done in one of the following ways if you are to be confident your presence has not impacted on the person's behaviour (meaning it would not be a true record of how their behaviour would usually be).

INCIDENTAL RECORDINGS: If you are normally in the persons immediate environment, you should be able to make some observations *incidentally*, in other words, as you go about your normal tasks you can watch for the target behaviour and write down your recordings discretely as you see the behaviour emitted. Take into account, this will not be the most accurate way – because as you are not able to monitor the person all the time, you may miss important information.

NATURALISTIC OBSERVATION: This is the more accurate way of observing a person's behaviour, and recording the behaviour with minimal effects on that person's behaviour. You will need to work out a position in the environment where you can clearly see the person, but also where your presence will either be unknown, or be unlikely to have any impact on the person's normal pattern of behaviour.

From the information collected in the questionnaire in case study one, some hypotheses (possibilities) can be formed.

1) Sarah is hungry? This is hypothesised from the information that Sarah emits the target behaviour more often around meal times.

2) Sarah is tired? Sarah's screaming behaviour is more often in the mornings, and part of the target behaviour sometimes includes "I want to go home", go home to sleep?

3) Sarah simply does not like being at the Art and Craft centre anymore? Is she bored with the activities offered?

*4) **Sarah is trying to get attention from staff?*** Even the responses *"Shut up"* and *"Please be quiet"* are forms of attention.

To help us now test the hypotheses to see what is the likely function of the behaviour, have a look at the table on the next page to see the categories of behaviour these hypotheses come into.

Example Description of Behaviour	Function Category
Sarah is hungry? *This is hypothesised from the information that Sarah emits the target behaviour more often around meal times* **Sarah is tired?** *Sarah's screaming behaviour is more often in the mornings, and part of the target behaviour sometimes includes "I want to go home", go home to sleep?*	**Wanting a tangible response/item** *- (food, bed to sleep on)*
Sarah simply does not like being at the Art and Craft centre anymore? *Is she bored with the activities offered?*	**Escaping task demand -** *(wants another activity, or environment)*
Sarah is trying to get attention from staff? *Even the responses "Shut up" and "Please be quiet" are forms of attention.*	**Attention Seeking**

Once you have formed a (or some) hypothesis, you now need to 'test' whether your hypothesis is correct. This is necessary as you need to be sure what you think the function of the behaviour is, is correct. This will then take you through to forming a strategy to reduce or at least manage the target behaviour.

Now we have the three hypotheses about what the function of the target behaviour (Sarah screaming) may be, we can test each one to see whether we are correct.

Obviously, to be able to really judge whether we are correct or not, we need to have an idea of how much screaming Sarah may emit in a certain period of time, when we know things are as per normal (that is, we have not made any changes to her environment or activities). In this example, we can select a 30 minute period in the morning just after Sarah arrives at the Art and Craft facility. We will observe Sarah, and ensure no one does anything out of the norm during this 30 minute period. Each time Sarah emits the target behaviour, make a mark on a table on a pad of paper. At the end of the thirty minutes, you can then count up how many times Sarah emitted the behaviour (you are making a baseline recording).

To ensure accuracy around these recordings, you need to have a specific definition of the behaviour. For example, does a scream lasting 2 seconds count, or only screams lasting over 5 seconds count? If there are two screams within 3 seconds of each other, does that count as one scream, or two? This is important, because if you are to test your hypotheses to see whether they are correct, you need an accurate record of the amount of behaviours emitted in a thirty minute period before any strategies are implemented (this is often called the baseline figure), and compare it to another thirty minute period with the hypotheses being tested.

In this example the target behaviour is defined as *"Any scream (high pitch squeal) emitted lasting 3 second or longer, with at least a 5 second space between screams. If another scream occurs within 5 seconds of the first scream, they will be counted as one scream."*

The baseline recordings showed Sarah screamed 13 times in the 30 minute period measured.

Below the hypotheses listed, is the method we used to test each hypothesis.

1) **Sarah is hungry.** This is hypothesised from the information that Sarah emits the target behaviour more often around meal times.

Just after Sarah arrives at the Art and Craft facility, she is given a snack of two muesli bars, this is in addition to her breakfast that she has had around thirty minutes prior to arriving there.

The same time period is measured (thirty minutes) on her arrival at the facility and after the muesli bars are eaten. There is one instance of screaming towards the end of the thirty minute period.

Every thirty minutes after Sarah arrives, she is offered a small snack of either a muesli bar, crackers, or piece of fruit. No further recordings are taken, but staff report a dramatic reduction in screaming.

2) **Sarah is tired.** Sarah's screaming behaviour is more often in the mornings, and part of the target behaviour sometimes includes *"I want to go home"*, go home to sleep?

Sarah is permitted to sleep in thirty minutes longer in the morning. The recordings are taken again for thirty minutes after arrival. Screams emitted 11 times. Sarah is offered the chance to 'nap' every three hours at the facility – but she declines the offers. Staff report no noticeable decrease in screaming for the day.

3) **Sarah simply does not like being at the Art and Craft centre anymore.** Is she bored with the activities offered?

New activities are offered to Sarah right from arrival until leaving. Screams emitted nine times in recording period. Staff report a slight decrease overall for the day.

4) **Sarah is trying to get attention from staff.** Even the responses *"Shut up"* and *"Please be quiet"* are forms of attention.

Staff are instructed NOT to make comments to Sarah during or within 2 minutes of screams emitted from Sarah. This means no prompts to 'be quiet', and no other verbal interactions. They are also asked that when Sarah is NOT screaming, they are to give lots of attention via verbal interaction, this includes *"How's it going Sarah"*, *"Hey that painting looks great Sarah!"*, *"Good to see you hear today"*, etc. Recording period showed *19 screams emitted. This strategy was trialed over three days, due to expecting what is referred to as an 'Extinction Burst' (read the chapter on Extinction to learn more about an 'extinction burst'). On the third day's recording period, with the strategy as outlined above being implemented each day, there were 2 screams emitted.

From the hypotheses tested, it can be seen that gaining a tangible item (food) is one likely function of Sarah's behaviour. When given an extra snack just after arriving at the facility, the amount of screams emitted reduced, as did the screaming for that day when regular snacks were offered (according to the anecdotal reports of staff).

The other function of her behaviour appears to be to get attention from staff. Though the initial amount of screaming increased on the first day's recording (as can be expected with extinction based strategies), it reduced substantially by the third day's recording.

Ensuring Your Findings are Correct

Of course there is always a chance the behaviour that appears to have 'changed' since you tested your hypothesis, has actually changed due to something other than what you had implemented. To give you some more assurance that you are on the right track with the strategy being trialed, you can remove the 'treatment' condition and see whether the behaviour increases again (that is, the strategy you are currently implementing, such as the snacks in the example, is stopped, to see whether the target behaviour returns again). Of course, you must consider the ethics of doing this. Would it be acceptable to stop an intervention that was reducing a behaviour that was harmful to the person it was aimed at, or harmful to others in the environment?

Remember, the information covered in this lesson is to give you only a brief overview about functional assessments, and unless you are entirely comfortable with what you are doing, and confident you have all the knowledge required, you would not normally attempt a functional assessment without professional guidance through each step.

BASIC CONSIDERATIONS OF BEHAVIOUR

The people who often take the brunt of unwanted behaviour from others, are those who provide the 'hands on' (or 'front line') support.

These people can be support workers, teachers, parents, siblings, or volunteers. Often they are expected to manage a person's unwanted behaviour, yet are not given the training to be able to do this safely or in a way that will reduce the frequency of those behaviours. This book is designed to empower these people with the basic knowledge and skills they need to do this. This chapter talks about 'hands-on' basics that will help increase your safety, and ensure the people you support are treated with respect and in a way that will (begin to) help them reduce the behaviours that may be affecting their quality of life.

Some of the most basic and what most would call common-sense aspects of supporting a person with unwanted behaviour are also sometimes the basics that seem to be forgotten. Some of these are listed below, give them some thought and ask yourself if you apply these as per the norm in your day to day interactions with supporting a person with unwanted behaviour.

- **Respect:** No matter whether someone's behaviour is at times unwanted or not, everyone deserves respect. Respect means more than just being 'politically correct' with what you say and how you say it. More so, it is interacting with that person for whom they are, not for the level of anxiety they may cause you at times. How many times have you seen someone avoid one person in particular, because in the past they have had an issue with them, or with their behaviour? Having respect when supporting someone with unwanted behaviour means putting whatever has happened in the past, in the past. That is, don't hold a person's historical behaviour against them now; don't bring up past incidents - as this in itself may trigger another incident. **We are working at improving the future, not punishing for the past.**

- **Modeling Appropriate Behaviour:** Having several years experience working in the behaviour specialist field, I would estimate that up to 30% of the families and support people I have worked with were at least partly to blame for the unwanted behaviours being emitted by the person who was referred to me. This may seem rather harsh, and maybe even simplistic, but let me explain why I say this. Some parents I worked with complained about their child often *"screaming and shouting"* at them and others whenever they didn't get there own way. During the same assessment, they often admitted that they *"shouted"* at the same child when they wouldn't do what they had asked - in other words, when the Parent didn't get their way they shouted at the child. Children most certainly learn large amounts of information that affect their behaviours from their environment. If a Parent, teacher, or other support person continually shouts at them, it is well supported that in many cases the child will eventually start emitting this same behaviour, as this is what they have seen their 'role models' do and so this must be an ok response. You have to work hard at modeling (displaying, demonstrating) the behaviour that should be emitted by those you support. Whether those people are children, adults with a disability, inmates, or others - **you need to monitor your own behaviour constantly, and adjust it where necessary.**

- **Look For and Reinforce Appropriate Behaviour:** At times we all reprimand others for behaviour that is inappropriate. Whether it be *"Don't play near the windows, it's dangerous",* or, *"Stop slouching in your chair",* many of these verbal prompts we make almost every day to help keep others safe. Prompting people about these things is not wrong. However, we also need to ensure we recognise when people we support behave appropriately, and reinforce that behaviour (increasing the chances it will be repeated in future). Let's look at a rather basic example. When a child takes it's first steps then falls over, what is the typical reaction of the Parent's/Caregivers? Do they praise the child - *"Fantastic, we are so happy you took three steps!"* to reinforce the behaviour, or do they look for the inappropriate behaviour only *"You fell over! You need to* try harder to walk without falling over, I am so disappointed!" Of course at least 99.9% of Parents and caregivers (and we would hope 100 %) praise the child for the walking, not punish for the falling over. We need to carry this principle into other aspects of life also. Some people may have the challenge that the person supported almost never seems to emit appropriate behaviour, so how can they reinforce it? To start off with, even if it is just one single minute where the person is behaving appropriately - reinforce that! *"Hey, it's so good to see you sitting quietly and listening, I am really pleased with you".* You may do this for every minute or more of appropriate behaviour 6 or 7 times each day to start with, then only reinforce that behaviour when it is at least 2 minutes long, and so on until you get hour long blocks. Sometimes the smaller the steps, the better the results.

- **Consistency of Approach and Working as a Team:** When you learnt your alphabet at school, was it by listening to and saying it over and over again? For most of us, this would have been how we learnt it. Imagine though if one teacher taught you the alphabet in this traditional sequence one day, then another teacher started in the middle of the alphabet the next day, and another taught it backwards the following day. It would have been very confusing, very hard to learn, and maybe even caused you to experience feelings of anxiety. You wouldn't have been sure which was the right way, and maybe would have given up altogether trying to learn it.

When teaching new behaviours or attempting to reduce the frequency of existing unwanted behaviours, consistency of approach is very important if success is to be reached. If one person allows TV watching for 20 minutes only after all toys are picked up, yet another person allows unlimited TV watching whether all toys are picked up or not, what is the rule to be followed? It is likely the person who enforces that TV watching is contingent on the picking up of toys will start experiencing some unwanted behaviour from that child when they next try to prompt them to follow the rule. On the other hand, the other person will not understand what the problem is (though also may be spending much of THEIR time picking up toys). This can also lead to strained relationship dynamics between family members and/or staff. All 'team' members should know the strategy being implemented, understand it, and agree that they will follow this strategy to detail. Regular meetings discussing progress, difficulties, and of course successes will help with consistency. **Always have agreement on any approach before you implement it, discuss progress regularly, and celebrate every success - no matter how small.**

SAFETY

SAFETY is of paramount concern for everyone involved in supporting people who at times emit unwanted behaviour.

Most organisations and individuals are well aware of legislation that governs the safety of individuals in the workplace. This chapter looks at all aspects of safety that affects us as individuals supporting people who may emit unwanted behaviour, and also the safety of those individuals themselves.

There are many aspects of safety that we need to consider, some of the more important are listed below, and we will examine each one in reasonable detail as you go through this chapter.

- **Privacy** - How can we keep a person's private details safe from others?

- **Cultural and Religious Beliefs** - People's cultural and religious safety can also be compromised, sometimes inadvertently.

- **Psychological and Physical Safety** - This applies to the people we are supporting, and to ourselves

- **Safety from Allegations** - Keep yourself safe from allegations of abuse or unprofessional conduct

Privacy

Debriefing is an important part of keeping stress levels low, working out better ways of handling difficult situations, and ensuring everyone has had their say about an incident. Professional debriefs usually achieve all these points, but so often a professional debrief just does not occur. Subsequently people often debrief their day's events in their own way; sometimes this is done by telling a partner, family member, or even a good friend about their day. This is where sometimes a persons' private details can slip out.

Letting your partner know that *"Johnny was smashing windows today"* seems innocent enough, but what happens when your partner 'innocently' mentions this to a friend at work, who tells another friend - who happens to be Johnny's Parent's neighbour, who goes on to tell the whole street about that *"terrible Johnny!"*? Suddenly your innocent comments have created a great deal of stress for 'Johnny' and his family, and compromised his safety at home and school.

Once you finish work for the day, you finish work for the day. In other words, what happens at work should stay at work, and also vice versa. **It is also dangerous to you to let out some personal details of your home life.** Some individuals may use these personal details against you at a later date. Those working in the Justice System are particularly at risk, as blackmail or threats may come from some information they have learned about you.

Of course if your partner is the only person you get the chance to debrief with, you can still do this – but ensure you never give out names or personal details about the people you support.

Cultural and Religious Beliefs

Everyone has the right to believe what it is that they hold special to themselves. Whether this is religious belief, or a cultural custom, they are entitled to this, and in fact should be welcomed into practicing this belief if this assists their wellbeing.

Infringing on a person's cultural or religious beliefs can jeopardise their safety. Imagine what would happen if a staff member at a school laughed at a young girl who insisted on not eating meat on a certain day of the week, making the comment *"How silly, it doesn't make any difference - forget about that nonsense."* Now other children also join in laughing at her and making rude remarks when she tries to stick to this rule that is a part of her religious belief. Suddenly her wellbeing at school is compromised, as is her relationship with her family when she begins to question the belief that she has always accepted and welcomed - up to now.

We do not have the right to judge the appropriateness or validity of another person's beliefs. If you feel that the belief may lead to endangering the person's safety, discuss this with the person themself, or their support people, to try and find a way for them to safely practice the belief. Always be respectful and non-judgmental.

Psychological Safety

Debriefing critical incidents is an important process if people's psychological wellbeing is to be protected. This applies to staff who support people with sometimes unwanted behaviour, and also to Parents and other family members who are sometimes involved in stressful situations.

A debrief does not necessarily have to be carried out by a professional *(though - if it is a very serious incident, or has caused an obviously high amount of stress/anxiety in one or more people, you should consider engaging the services of a*

Psychologist or someone trained and qualified in providing psychological debriefs). A debrief consists of discussing an incident that has happened recently (though the incident should be completely over - i.e. there should not still be anyone actively upset or angry). What happened exactly, who was there, who was involved, what could be done to prevent another similar incident, what can be done better next time, how does everyone feel about what happened? Ensure everyone involved in the incident is involved in the debrief meeting (except the instigator of the incident if it is likely to get them angry or overly upset having to discuss the incident in this setting). Everyone should get their say, but do not use this process to lay blame or judge others actions. It is a process for people to let others know how they felt things went, and to let them have their say (Though again, I stress it is not a time to pick on anyone or victimise people, more so a way of looking at ways to improve things, and/or to let go of anything people are hanging on to psychologically).

This course is not to teach you how to provide specialist debriefing, but more so to highlight the importance of the debrief process, and that often a talk at the end of each day between the team (whether that team be Husband and Wife, Teacher and Teacher Aid, or Support Staff) can meet the needs of this process.

Look after yourself properly, to support others properly. Ensuring you get enough sleep, eat healthy, and get adequate exercise are all important if you wish to be able to deal with sometimes stressful situations that may occur each day. If you start the day supporting someone with unwanted behaviour when you are already tired, have low energy, or have had a 'bad night' you will struggle to support them in a way that is helpful, and may not be able to put into practice what you have learnt from this book and from your experience of appropriate support.

When a person is elevated in behaviour, do not get into a power struggle with them. You need to be aware of some psychological aspects in regards to your safety. A 'Power Struggle' is when a person starts to challenge your authority, such as *"Who says YOU can tell ME what to do!?"* If you now begin to raise your voice, speak in an intimidating manner, or use threatening body language (such as invading the persons personal space) they will usually escalate their behaviour, also now shouting just a little (or maybe a lot) louder than you, they will start trying to intimidate you back. Remember, they want to try and be the boss. So instead of raising your voice, stay calm, repeat your request again calmly, don't answer the *"Who made you the boss"* type questions because you don't need to. All you need to do is to get across the request you are making.

"Stay firm, but calm."

Safety from Allegations

Allegations of inappropriate or threatening behaviour from a person supported against a support person, teacher, or even a parent are unfortunately not that uncommon. Of course sometimes these allegations are substantiated and the support person is dealt with by the legal system, but other times the allegations are untrue. Though the allegation may be shown to be untrue, the emotional scars it can leave can last a very long time. Often a person's future confidence and nervous disposition is effected.

There are certain precautions people who support others with sometimes unwanted behaviour can take to minimise the risk of false accusations. These standard precautions are listed below:

- **Two people = a witness, One person = a risk.** If a person's behaviour has become challenging, it is always best to have a second person monitoring the intervening person's interactions. That is, have a witness (as well as them being a back up person to assist if needed) to what happens when you intervene in an attempt to de-escalate a potentially harmful situation.

- **What does go on behind closed doors?** If you need to interact with a person in their or your room, or in a room where no one else is present, at the very least - leave the door open.

- **Keep your hands to yourself?** As soon as you physically touch someone, you run the risk of being accused of one of two things. 1 - You assaulted them, or 2 - you touched them inappropriately. I usually suggest you keep at least a leg-length distance away from the people you support (naturally a Parent – child relationship is different, appropriate touching is important). Of course touch is important to all people, as is the need to sometimes physically prompt or comfort someone, but when these interactions are not needed - **remember the one-leg-length rule.**

- **Mind Your Language.** If you always keep your language free from swear words, sarcasm, and threats of punishment, you will lessen the chances of being accused of saying anything untoward. Act professionally, and with compassion but firmness, and people are more likely to respect you and less likely to accuse you of inappropriate behaviour. Also remember that you are modeling appropriate behaviour through what you say, and how you say it. The person is learning from you all the time. Parents need to be particularly mindful of their tone of voice and their choice of words. Your child's personality is being formed in their early years by what they hear and see around them, particularly from their parents / guardians.

EXTINCTION

WHAT IS EXTINCTION?

Extinction in behavioural science is the term given to ceasing a response that has in the past been given after an unwanted behaviour was emitted.

So, what does this mean? As discussed earlier in the book, what occurs immediately after a behaviour has occurred is a response.

For example, you loose your pen at work; you swear out loud because you have lost it, and your workmates laugh. The laughing was the direct response (or response that has stimulus control) to your swearing. You now know that in future your workmates are likely to laugh when you swear, which they do. However, after repeating this behaviour again and again your workmates grow weary of it. Subsequently, they decide to put this swearing behaviour from you on extinction. Each time you swear at work in future no one laughs or comments. You wonder why, maybe they didn't hear you? You do it louder and more frequent, still no laughing or comments to the swearing behaviour. After a while you cease to swear as you no longer receive the response you used to enjoy receiving after you emitted that behaviour.

There are some important stages in the example above that relate to the extinction process. Did you recognise them? They were the following:

- **Behaviour identified:** We identified the behaviour in question (or target behaviour) as swearing at work around your workmates.

- **Reinforcing response identified:** We identified the response that seemed to maintain the target behaviour: Laughing from the workmates after they heard the swearing.

- **Behaviour put onto extinction:** In this case, the workmates stopped the laughing and also did not make any direct comments related to the swearing behaviour.

- **Extinction Burst:** The swearing became louder and more frequent. This is common with a behaviour when first put onto extinction; it becomes more frequent and intense. This is termed the extinction burst. Often visually represented by a graph similar to a bell graph – the frequency and intensity of the behaviour being emitted is a stable fairly regular amount, then an increase is seen when put on extinction, then dropping to a lower level or ceasing after a period of time (there is no set time, it differs with each individual, the specific behaviour being emitted and how long that behaviour has been emitted for by that person in the past). Another way of looking at this is to think of a child who always gets a sweet when they ask for one, but one day you run out of sweets – so they ask more and more, and get louder and louder – this increase in the frequency and intensity of the 'asking behaviours' is an extinction burst.

One thing missing from the example however was an appropriate behaviour being taught to replace the behaviour put on extinction. This is a common mistake, and one that you should be aware of when following strategies that may have been designed by behaviour specialists, or alike. If there is not a plan in place to teach and reinforce an alternative behaviour that will serve the same function as the behaviour put on extinction - ask the question. Remember some of the so-called specialists are not necessarily that well trained (if trained in the science of behaviour at all). In fact, does the behavioural therapist know what the function of the behaviour they are trying to stop is? Did they do a functional assessment? In the example above, the function of the swearing (the continued swearing) appeared to be to receiving positive attention (reinforcement) by way of laughing from workmates. Maybe it could be suggested that this person tells suitable jokes at appropriate times to receive laughing instead of the inappropriate swearing?

RISKS OF USING AN EXTINCTION BASED STRATEGY

Though putting an unwanted behaviour on extinction is a common and usually successful strategy, it does come with some risks. There are also times when using the extinction approach is not recommended. We look at both these issues below.

- **Possible Aggression:** When behaviour is put onto extinction, the person who was emitting the behaviour will experience increased anxiety due to not receiving the response they found reinforcing in the past. With anxiety, comes the increased risk that the person will behave in a way to try and force the person to give the response they used to. This may include the risk of physical and/or verbal aggression. Again, introducing an alternative wanted behaviour that will allow the person to receive a similar response (now an appropriate response) will help lessen the chance of aggression occurring.

- **New Behaviour Is Emitted (more challenging than the original):** Another risk is the possibility a new behaviour, also unwanted, starts to be emitted in an attempt to get the original reinforcing responses to return. For example, a person who used to *slap themselves (not hard enough to cause any real harm) now bites themselves, drawing blood at times and resulting in support people having to respond. (*Note the information at the end of this chapter relating to extinction and self injurious behaviour).

- **Extinction Strategies Should NOT Be Used For Self Injurious Behaviour (S.I.B.):** As explained above, there is a risk when placing an unwanted behaviour on extinction that a new behaviour may start to be emitted by the person. With S.I.B. there is a risk that the harmful behaviour currently emitted, is replaced by a more damaging behaviour - remember the person wants to receive the response they used to receive. For example, slapping their own face may change to banging their face against a corner of a table, etc. For this reason *do NOT use extinction based strategies with people emitting self injurious behaviour UNLESS the strategy has been implemented by a behaviour specialist who is also closely monitoring the strategy, and has safety mechanisms in place in case a more risky behaviour starts to be emitted.*

- **Consistency:** Unless all the people who support the person with the unwanted behaviour that is being placed on extinction are consistent in following the extinction strategy, it is unlikely you will have any success. Have another look at the example given at the start of this lesson, and now factor in what you believe would happen if there was one person who continued to laugh at the swearing behaviour? It is likely that you either would have targeted that person specifically with the swearing, as they still laughed, meaning that others (although they no longer laughing at your swearing) also had to be recipients of the unwanted behaviour as they continue to overhear it. Now take this to another environment with a different behaviour and different person emitting the behaviour. Do you believe they are likely to reduce the behaviour or stop the behaviour if one person still reacts?

DESENSITISATION

This chapter looks at ways to help desensitise a person to a particular stimuli, action, or event.

If a person refuses to wear a hat of any sort, and becomes obviously upset (may scream, cover their head with their hands, become extremely angry) we can densensitise them to the wearing of hats. If a person insists on clinging to another person whenever they walk on a concrete path, but are fine everywhere else, you can help desensitise them to walking on concrete paths. There are of course hundreds of other possibilities (including reducing phobias such as agoraphobia (fear of enclosed spaces), or even a fear of dogs or heights).

Often reducing an irrational response to a certain stimuli (such as an apparent fear of, or irrational dislike of wearing headphones) will help you with progressing with a specific behavioural strategy to modify another behaviour. The fact you discovered the person had a fear or strong dislike of a certain stimuli or event has probably come from the information you have gathered in your observations of the target behaviour/s, or from other observations. However, you need to be sure that the 'fear' or 'strong dislike' is not part of an escapance behaviour (escaping task demand), because if it is - this may change things. In the next paragraph I give an example of this.

Jack refuses to put his winter jacket on each morning. When his parents try to encourage him to put it on, due to the very cold weather in the area they live in, he runs to his room and tries to hold his door shut preventing anyone from entering. This behaviour has only been occurring for the last six weeks, and before this he always wore his jacket without a problem. Jack's parents believe he has formed *"some sort of phobia"* about wearing his jacket, and so would like information on desensitising him to his jacket.

After some questioning of Jack's Parents, it is discovered that just over six weeks ago a new boy started at school who it appears has been teasing Jack. It also became apparent that the first time he refused to wear his jacket his father let him stay home from school as he was afraid he would get very sick going through the day without his jacket.

After some observations of Jack in the morning, and the Parents introducing a different jacket, the behaviour continues - but a hypothesis is formed about the function of this behaviour. It is determined that this behaviour is very unlikely to be due to a phobia, but is instead a learned behaviour that helps Jack escape task demand. In this case the task demand he was escaping was that of going to school and keeping away from the boy who teased him. Jack had learnt that when he left for school in the morning, he always put his jacket on first, so he thought that if he did not put his jacket on, then he would not have to go to school. This behaviour was reinforced (negatively reinforced because a response he did not like, that of having to go to school, was removed) inadvertently by his Dad the first time by allowing Jack to stay home from school. **Remember, what happens immediately after a behaviour is emitted determines the likelihood of that behaviour being repeated in the future.**

If the behaviour of concern was around the behaviour emitted when attempting to prompt the person to wear a sunhat (which may be a necessity on a hot summer day), and after assessment it was found to be an irrational fear of hat wearing, we can use a desensitisation process.

The 'fear' or avoidance of wearing hats (or other similar stimuli like certain clothes, scarves, sunglasses, etc) may be due to the person feeling uncomfortable with the tactile sensation of something on their head, or it may be they fear it will cover their eyes and they won't be able to see, or there could be another quite reasonable explanation.

The challenge is to introduce those stimuli in a hierarchical manner. This means, don't try and rush the person with the 'full-on treatment' (known as flooding). In this example - you should not keep persisting to put the hat on the persons head when they are obviously emitting behaviour that indicates they are very unhappy about having it on. Instead, we will look at a gradual process of introducing the least disturbing stimuli and interaction with those stimuli gradually, and progress this in a systematic way. Look at the following table for this example:

Week One	Show pictures of hats (not on)
Week Two	Show pictures of people wearing hats
Week Three	Show person some real hats, from a distance - including people putting them on
Week Four	Show person hats, and putting one on yourself, next to them
Week Five	Encourage person to hold a hat (or even just touch one to start with)
Week Six	Lightly touch persons head with a piece of material - for 4-5 seconds, to start with, or what they appear to cope with
Week Seven	Place a hat on the persons head - just let it sit lightly.
Week Eight	Prompt person to place hat on their head
Week Nine	***Should now be desensitised to hat wearing.***

Note that the example just given would be for a person who had an extreme fear of hat wearing, and it had been established the fear appeared to be hats themselves rather than a trying to escape a particular task. You may also find you are able to speed this process up, or slow it down according to how well the person appears to be coping.

The same approach could be used for a fear of dogs. Show pictures of dogs, then maybe videos, then a real dog in the distance, then close up, gently patting the dog at arms length, and so on.

> *The chapter on Toilet Training gives some specific examples of desensitising a child to using a toilet. You may want to jump to this chapter now and read those examples if you want to enhance your knowledge around desensitisation.*

As you have read, sometimes what many people would take for granted becomes a 'big deal' for others. Being non-judgemental is an important part of working successfully on reducing unwanted behaviours. If we were to decide the behaviour is *"just silly"* we will not be able to work in a systematic and consistent manner. If this is the case then success is unlikely because consistency and an analytic approach is needed to follow through with behavioural strategies.

Note: *Some people with Autism may have extreme sensory sensitivity to some stimuli, and so trying to desensitise them may not actually be an option – though possible, it will usually be a much more difficult and more detailed approach than what I have discussed. Read the chapter on autism for further information.*

WHAT IS REINFORCEMENT

Reinforcement is an event or action that takes place immediately after a wanted (or appropriate) behaviour has been emitted, that increases the likelihood of that behaviour being repeated again in the future. Reinforcement can also be provided at a later time, if linked by what we call a 'bridging reinforcer' (though it is preferable, and certainly more effective if the reinforcer occurs as soon as possible after the behaviour is emitted).

Positive Reinforcement

Positive reinforcement refers to something (a tangible **(touchable)** item, a special event, or verbal praise) given to the person who emitted the behaviour to increase the likelihood of that behaviour being repeated in the future.

The item, special event or verbal praise must be given immediately (preferably within seconds) of the behaviour being emitted for it to have maximum effect. Let's look at some examples of positive reinforcement (shown in italic) in the examples below.

- **Joe puts away his toys when first asked** - *"Great job Joe, extra TV time for you"*. The verbal praise *"great job Joe"* is the positive reinforcer, with the *"extra TV time"* also acting as a positive reinforcer.

- **Susan hands in her financial report on time - *The Boss shakes her hand, and says "Great job Susan, I'm impressed".*** The hand shake and the verbal praise are positive reinforcers.
- **Harry, who has an intellectual disability, goes fifteen minutes without hitting others - *Music is switched on.*** The music itself acts as the positive reinforcer here. Referring to what the behaviour is that is being reinforced is actually not necessary, as the person will pair what happens after the behaviour with the behaviour itself (sometimes more than one instance of pairing the target behaviour-reinforcer will be required though).

Positive (or negative) reinforcement is the most important aspect of teaching or modifying any behaviour. To increase the probability of a wanted behaviour occurring again in the future a positive (or negative – *read below*) reinforcer must be present after the behaviour is first emitted. So to modify a behaviour, that is, to change an unwanted behaviour to a wanted behaviour, there needs to be reinforcement of the wanted behaviour and no reinforcement occurring for the unwanted behaviour. An example of this would be an employee who continually arrives late to work; subsequently he does not receive his weekly bonus. The week he does arrive to work on time each day, he does receive his bonus. Teaching a new wanted behaviour follows the same principle. An infant learning how to walk, she takes her first two steps and the Mother immediately cuddles, kisses her, and tells her how good she is - the walking behaviour has just been reinforced by the Mother's praise, meaning the infant wants to repeat the behaviour again.

Imagine what would happen if when an infant was taking its first steps, then fell and the Parents rushed to it and shouted at it for falling rather than praising it for walking. The learning to walk process would be considerably slowed if it happened at all.

All behaviours follow the same basic principles; they need to be reinforced if the likelihood of that behaviour being repeated in the future is to be increased.

Negative Reinforcement

Negative reinforcement refers to a condition that is removed or avoided that increases the likelihood of the behaviour being repeated again in the future. Negative reinforcement is often mistaken as a type of punishment, but it is not. The fact that is it referred to reinforcement infers it results in increasing the likelihood of the behaviour being repeated again.

Again, this type of reinforcement should also occur immediately after the behaviour has been emitted.

Some examples of negative reinforcement (shown in italic) are:

- **Harry has three pages of school work to finish before he can have his break.** As Harry has been working steadily, without interrupting others (which was the target behaviour to change) the teacher removes one of his pages of school work. *"You don't need to do this one page Harry as you have worked so well without interrupting others, great job!"*
- **Mary dislikes sitting at her desk doing her homework,** and would much rather be able to do her work at the dining room table. Today she has sat and stayed on task, so her *Mother removes the rule about having to do her homework at her desk*, and allows her to finish her work at the dining room table.
- **You leave work early to avoid traffic delays.** *The lower traffic volume* encourages you to leave early again on future occasions.

As seen in the examples, it was the removal of a rule or condition that resulted in there being a benefit to the person whose behaviour is being targeted for change. Subsequently, the likelihood of them repeating that wanted behaviour in the future has increased.

So What Is Punishment?

A punishment decreases the likelihood of the behaviour being repeated in the future.

This author does not endorse or recommend punishment based methods of behaviour modification, however you should understand what punishment (also referred to as aversive type strategies) is, how it works, and why it is not a preferred method of modification for unwanted behaviour.

Though behaviour specialists may sometimes resort to an aversive strategy as a last resort, the following considerations must be taken into account.

- **Punishment based strategies often have only short term effects**

- **Resentment from the person who received the punishment towards the person punishing them is common, meaning a future workable relationship will be difficult**

- **A power struggle between the two parties can quickly and easily develop**

Some *Myths* about Punishment

Punishment is only when some physical act (such as a smack or slap) takes place. This is not correct; punishment is any act or withdrawal of an expected stimulus in an attempt to reduce the chances of an unwanted behaviour occurring in the future.

Time-Out is not a punishment. This is also incorrect. Time-out means being placed in, or directed to an area away from reinforcers (stimuli that the person prefers to be interacting with). So - the fact something has been withdrawn or limited makes time-out a punishment. 'Time-Out', as seen on some of the pop-psychology type programmes on TV, is not used properly. Though we do not endorse the use of 'Time-Out', if it is to be used as a last resort strategy it should at least be used properly. If it is to be used, the child should be placed in an area that is free from items that they find to be reinforcing. For example, it is hardly a workable strategy if the child is simply placed in their bedroom, where all their toys and books are. Instead, they should be placed in an area free from toys, books, TV, games, etc. The area should also be safe, so there is no access to poisons, or other harmful objects. We suggest the bathroom, but **with the door open**, so the parent or support person can still keep an eye on them to ensure their safety *(also double check they can not access medicines or poisons)*. Again – we do not recommend the use of 'Time Out', but if it is used **NEVER PLACE YOUR CHILD IN A ROOM WITH THE DOOR CLOSED.** If they continually leave the room before the designated 'Time Out' period is up, simply place them back in the room with no fuss, no comments and using a minimal and safe physical escort type approach.

Anti-punishment advocates are just being politically correct, and have no real evidence to back their claims that punishment is really harmful. Though it is true some anti-punishment lobbyists may push their views more for political gain rather than through their understanding of behaviour modification, there is evidence that some punishment based strategies can be both harmful and have only short term effects on the target behaviour.

Selecting Reinforcers

The reinforcers you will use to reinforce the wanted behaviour need to be selected carefully as they need to be items or events that the person with the targeted behaviour actually will find pleasurable to receive. For example, if after you finished your weeks work, your Boss gave you a basket full of carrots instead of your standard pay it is likely (unless you are addicted to carrots and find the receipt of them a life-long-must) that you will not be keen on working again next week. However, if you found the receipt of gold diamond studded jewelry rewarding, it is likely that your behaviour would be reinforced if your boss handed you a bag full of that at the end of your week.

So, how do you know what will and won't reinforce a wanted behaviour? This can be particularly tricky if the person whose behaviour is being targeted can not communicate as well as others. To aid this reinforcement process there are some systems you can use.

Direct - For People Who Can Communicate Effectively:
Simply ask the person, offering a selection of choices, what they would most like to receive? For example, if it was an adult: What

would you like to receive the most - money, a CD, drive in the car, listening to music? Or other selections that you know from your knowledge (or other people's knowledge of the person) they like.

Direct - For People Who Can Not Communicate Effectively: Decide on what you believe the person enjoys receiving, again these items may include money, favourite food, time with a preferred object, listening to music, etc. Present the potential reinforcers to the person two at a time (if not the items themselves, then in visual form (photos or similar). The item the person chooses from each two presented should be put aside. Keep presenting the objects two at a time, until you have an equal number of non-selected items, and selected items. Now present the items from the selected pile two at a time, using the same system as before. When you finally get down to two or three items in your selected items pile, these will be your reinforcers to use in your strategy.

Other Support People: Other people who know the person, whose behaviour is being targeted for change, should be able to provide valuable information on what they believe would be suitable reinforcers. This is particularly helpful if the person has a disability that makes communication difficult, or their behaviour is so challenging that even a preference assessment as outlined above would be very difficult to conduct.

When selecting reinforcers you do need to keep in mind the appropriateness of the reinforcers you decide on using. Using candy, chocolate, or other unhealthy options in food reinforcers **is**

not recommended. Other reinforcers such as cigarettes and alcohol are definitely out of the question. It is hard to argue that teaching a new wanted behaviour, while affecting someone's physical health is acceptable. However, if all other choices of reinforcers are not successful and you know candy would be, do not rule it out completely. Do keep in mind though that you can also **flood** (also known as satiation) a person with reinforcers, meaning they hold little value in future. For example, if you do need to resort to using candy, one *m+m* is plenty - a handful is too much. The person needs to want to receive more of the reinforcer; they won't be if they have had more than enough after the first reinforcement takes place.

You also need to keep in mind how realistic the reinforcers that you choose are in regards to the longer term supply of them. Though you will not have to supply the same reinforcer permanently, because you will pair a secondary reinforcer with it (as discussed later in this chapter) if you choose a dollar coin as the first reinforcer to use, things could get very expensive very quickly.

The reinforcer you use does not need to be something the person keeps hold of. That is, it may be a special toy that the child plays with for say 30 seconds or a minute. It may be access to a favourite song on a CD player.

PAIRING PRIMARY AND SECONDARY REINFORCERS

It is important to pair your primary reinforcer (such as the toy access, favourite song, m+m, etc) with a secondary reinforcer. A secondary reinforcer is something that can be easily continued into the future. For example, the classic and common secondary reinforcer is verbal praise such as *"Well done"*, *"Great job"*, *"I am so pleased with you"*. It may be that with some behaviour you are reinforcing, verbal praise by itself may be enough. This is particularly so if the person receiving the reinforcement receives little positive verbal comments normally, and/or responds well to verbal praise.

To pair the primary reinforcer, with the secondary reinforcer, simply provide both at the same time, for example:

"Great job Joseph! Here is your special toy to play with. You have done so well!"

As the wanted behaviour happens more often, you can slowly fade the primary reinforcer, and just provide the secondary reinforcer. As the behaviour becomes more regular, you can also start fading the secondary reinforcer such as only providing it every second time, third time, then randomly.

Bridging Reinforcers

Sometimes you may find that providing an immediate positive reinforcement is not possible due to the logistics of the situation. For example, if the wanted behaviour to be reinforced is the person staying quiet while a lesson is presented, and there are numerous other students in the class, it may be that you need to delay the reinforcer until after the lesson is finished. However, as you will now understand, if the reinforcer is to be truly effective, it needs to be presented as soon as possible after the behaviour is emitted. To combat this problem a bridging reinforcer can be used.

A bridging reinforcer links the behaviour for reinforcement with the actual reinforcer, when the reinforcer can not be given immediately. That is, if there is a reason you can not provide the reinforcement for the behaviour immediately, another response occurs that will link the time gap between behaviour and the reinforcement. For example:

Walking through the supermarket with a child who, when they behave well in the shop, gets to stay up an extra 15 minutes, may have a bridging reinforcer of a red card that the Parent gives the child after a period of time in the shop. The child hands that card (the bridging reinforcer) to the Parent later that night for their 15 minutes extra time to stay up. The next page shows a table with an example of how a bridging reinforcer strategy can be put into practice.

Below is a table showing an example of how bridging reinforcers work

The Behaviour	The Challenge
Thomas has been disruptive in class, and we are now teaching him the wanted behaviour of *"no talking during lessons"*.	Due to there being only one teacher on duty in the class, she can not reinforce every two minutes of quiet behaviour (as was the initial strategy).
The Modified Strategy	**The Analysis**
Thomas is told before his lesson that as soon as he has ten ticks on his chart (displayed on the corner of the blackboard) he will receive ten minutes on the computer (the reinforcer that he enjoys). Now, for every two minutes of no talking, the teacher simply ticks a box on the table on the whiteboard as she continues to deliver the lesson. As the lesson only lasts twenty minutes, if Thomas has had ten lots of two minutes of "no talking behaviour", by the time the lesson is finished he will get his ten minutes computer time.	Thomas had his behaviour reinforced immediately by way of the ticks, yet the actual reinforcer he was wanting to earn was the computer time. The ticks acted as bridging reinforcers to link up the wanted behaviour with the preferred reinforcer. Another way this could have been done, was by a light being turned on and left on once the wanted behaviour was emitted, with the reinforcer being delivered at the end of the lesson if the light was on.

Another more common example of a bridging reinforcer is the time-sheets that some people have to fill in each day. Though you only receive your pay each fortnight or month (the reinforcer for your work), filling in your hours each day links your behaviour (work) with the reinforcer (pay).

Use of Reward Charts

There is much debate about the effectiveness of reward charts (like star charts, token systems, and similar). Some argue they can be very effective, others say they are of no use. This author believes that reward charts and token systems can be effective as bridging reinforcers if used correctly.

If the same principles are used in the giving of the star, token, tick (whatever is being used to fill the chart, or for the person to hand back in exchange for a preferred reinforcer) as apply to reinforcement generally, they should be an effective part of a behaviour modification strategy.

The following points are the most important if using a reward chart system (based on a simple star chart):

- **Start small.** That is, to start with let the person only have to emit a small number of instances of the wanted behaviour to receive enough stars to get access to the preferred reinforcer. For example, the wanted behaviour may be 'no hitting - periods of time', that is - you are trying to encourage longer and longer periods of time the person goes without hitting, by reinforcing periods of no-hitting. You may start with just three periods of five minutes of no hitting, giving the person a star on the chart after each five minutes. The next time you run the strategy, you may want to make it 5 stars equals' access to the reinforcer, slowly increasing the length of the periods of time and the amount of stars to receive.

- **Be Realistic.** Like goals, expectations of a change in behaviour must be realistic. If you wanted to use tokens to stop self injurious behaviour giving a token for no hurting self for a whole day and the person having to earn ten tokens before they get access to a favourite drink, is unrealistic. A token for no hurting self for 30 minutes, and having to get 2 tokens to get a favoured drink would be more realistic.

Reinforcement Schedules

Knowing what reinforcement schedules are, and having a basic understanding how different schedules can be utilised in behaviour modification and management strategies is important. However, there is a lot of in-depth knowledge required to fully understand the implementation of some of them. This chapter will provide basic information about the more commonly used schedules of reinforcement.

So what is a reinforcement schedule? A reinforcement schedule is a predetermined pattern of when a reinforcer will be given for the wanted behaviours emitted. That is, certain criteria have been established for when (how often) a reinforcer is given to the person who emits the behaviour that has been identified as the target wanted behaviour. This may make more sense after you read the brief definitions for the following reinforcement schedules, then look at the examples provided in the table.

FIXED RATIO SCHEDULE (FR): Here the reinforcer is given after a set number of times the wanted behaviour is emitted. For example, every third time the wanted behaviour is emitted it is reinforced.

CONTINUOUS RATIO SCHEDULE (CR): In a CR schedule each time the wanted behaviour is emitted, it is reinforced.

FIXED INTERVAL SCHEDULE (FI): A fixed interval schedule has a reinforcer delivered after a set interval of time since the last reinforcer was given. For example, the reinforcer is given the next time the wanted behaviour is emitted thirty minutes after the last reinforcer was given.

VARIABLE RATIO SCHEDULE (VR): Here the reinforcer is delivered after a random number of times the wanted behaviour is emitted, based on an average number of responses. That is, for example every 3rd time the wanted behaviour is emitted (on average) it will be reinforced. So, it may be the 5th time, then the 2nd, then the 4th, etc.

VARIABLE INTERVAL SCHEDULE (VI): With a VI schedule a reinforcer is delivered at random amounts of time after a wanted behaviour is emitted, based on a predetermined average time period.

Fixed Ratio Schedule	*Alex is given 20 cents for every third correct answer on his spelling homework.*
Continuous Ratio Schedule	*Alex is given 10 cents for every correct answer he gets on his spelling homework*
Fixed Interval Schedule	*Alex is given 50 cents after his first correct answer, then after two minutes, and his next correct answer, he gets another 50 cents, and so on.*
Variable Ratio Schedule	*Alex is given 20 cents after his first correct answer, then his 4th correct answer, then his 7th, then his 9th. On average he will be given his reinforcer (20 cents) every 3rd correct answer.*

Variable Interval Schedule	Alex is given 50 cents after his first answer, then after 3 minutes and his next correct answer another 50 cents, then after 2 minutes and his next correct answer another 50 cents, and so on. On average every two and a half minutes after a reinforcer is given, and another correct answer is provided he will receive 50 cents.

As can be seen in the table, different types of schedules of reinforcement can be used in different circumstances. That is, some are better with some types of behaviour than others.

More than one type of schedule can also be combined. These are referred to as **Compound Schedules of Reinforcement.** Have a look at the example below to give you an idea of when this may be useful:

Sally finds washing her hands after toileting a real challenge. Often when her support people try and encourage her to wash her hands after toileting, she will scream and cry, and try and avoid the hand washing behaviour. It has been suggested by a behaviour consultant to use two schedules of positive reinforcement to encourage hand washing. **The first is a continuous ratio schedule of reinforcement**, where every time Sally washes her hands after toileting she is given access to a tactile object she likes to hold and interact with for one minute. **There is also a fixed ratio schedule of reinforcement**, where after every third time Sally washes her hands, in addition to the tactile object, she will be given 5 minutes access to the sensory room. The reasoning behind this is firstly the fading of the access to the tactile object will be made easier as Sally will become accustomed to the sensory room access also after washing, and so staff can use that reinforcement only after the hand washing is more of a habit for Sally. That habit will be formed by the continuous schedule of reinforcement to start with.

Fading Reinforcers

Obviously reinforcers can not be given permanently at the rate that may initially be required to encourage a wanted behaviour. This is why a technique called **fading** must be used to reduce the frequency of reinforcers supplied.

Fading should only be introduced once the behaviour has started to become a habit. That is, the person is now emitting the behaviour on occasions other than just when they receive the reinforcer, and/or is showing competence and ease with emitting that wanted behaviour. This is where schedules of reinforcement have their part in a behavioural strategy. A fixed ratio or variable ratio schedule of reinforcement allows for wanted behaviours to go non-reinforced as well as have some reinforced. **When the behaviour is emitted regularly on the non-reinforced occasions, you can now start to increase the occurrences where you DO NOT reinforce it (this is fading the reinforcers).**

For example: Jim was receiving a "great job" verbal reinforcement on every second occasion that he threw his paper cutting rubbish directly in the bin. As he now performs this wanted behaviour on every occasion of paper cutting whether it is reinforced or not, his support person starts reinforcing randomly, every 3rd occasion, then 5th occasion, then only one in every 10-12 correct responses, and then only for **maintenance** (once every day or two).

Fading of reinforcers is an important part of any successful behavioural strategy. Without using fading, either a sudden end to reinforcement, or no end to reinforcement can bring obvious problems. Fade at a rate that is maintaining the wanted behaviour. This is where having statistics around how many correct responses (occurrences of wanted behaviour) occur in set time periods (per hour, two hours, or per day - whatever is most relevant) will allow you to measure whether fading is happening too quickly. If you see the wanted behaviours lessening, you may need to increase your frequency of reinforcement, and fade again at a slower rate. Keeping written records showing the amount of wanted behaviours emitted and amount of reinforcers given will aid in managing this process. Though it may be time consuming, and seem an unnecessary task, it may save you time and frustration in the long run. Having written records of your strategy may also assist others in future who may face the same challenges.

Maintenance

Maintenance of a wanted behaviour is sometimes needed if you believe it is a real possibility the behaviour may stop occurring in the near future. To provide maintenance of a wanted behaviour, simply provide reinforcement on occasion once your main reinforcement period has been faded. That is, at random times you can verbally reinforce the persons wanted behaviour *"Great job, you sure know how to do that well now"*. Or you may like to give the person an occasional special reinforcement of a treat for morning tea, being allowed to play early, have an extra tea break, etc. You may only need to do this once every week at a random time, where as you may have initially been reinforcing the behaviour after every time it was emitted. Again ensure these reinforcements happen as soon after the wanted behaviour is emitted as possible, so the person links that reinforcement with the behaviour.

REDUCING UNWANTED BEHAVIOURS

As discussed in earlier chapters - Before we decide on whether a behaviour falls into the unwanted behaviour or wanted behaviour categories, you need to remember that if a behaviour is to be chosen for modification it needs to be established why that behaviour is unwanted. That is, who is it who does not want that behaviour to be emitted, who decided it needs to be modified and why? For example, when a person tugs on another persons clothing to let them know they need to use the toilet, as they can not speak or know how to sign - is this an unwanted behaviour? It could be argued either way, but the criteria that should be used is:

Does this behaviour cause harm to the person concerned (including, does it stigmatise them)?

OR

Does this behaviour cause harm to others?

If the answer is yes to either of these questions, then it is likely that it is an unwanted behaviour that needs to be modified.

As can be seen on the last page, you need to be sure the behaviour that you or others have decided is an unwanted behaviour really qualifies for falling into this category.

Strategies for reducing an unwanted behaviour usually focus on one of two approaches, or a combination of the two. Firstly placing the behaviour on extinction is one approach. The second more common method is introducing another behaviour that is either a desirable alternative behaviour, or is an incompatible behaviour. Let's look at some examples of these strategies before discussing them in greater detail.

Placing a Behaviour on Extinction

Jonathon continually screams when he is hungry, and will scream until he receives something to eat. Over time his support people have learned that the quicker they get him food, the quicker he will stop screaming. A Behavioural Therapist has advised them to ignore this unwanted behaviour. That is, do not react to the screaming whatsoever. Do not look at him, talk to him, or interact in any way with him while he is screaming. Above all, they are told, do not give him food while he is screaming. This strategy was referred to as 'placing the behaviour on extinction'.

Introducing an Alternative Behaviour

As in the previous example, Jonathon's screaming when hungry has become an unwanted behaviour. Another Behavioural Therapist has suggested teaching Jonathon to use a hunger card visual when he wants food, and to reinforce its use to get him used to this. Staff give Jonathon the visual (a small laminated card with a picture of a cookie and a sandwich on it). The first few times they give it to Jonathon, he simply throws it on the floor. They wait until he appears to be getting hungry, but before he begins screaming, they hand him the card again, then straight away take it from his hand and hand him a plate with a sandwich and a cookie on it. They do this several times until he associates exchanging the visual card for food.

Introducing an Incompatible Behaviour

Jane enjoys carrying her soft toys around everywhere with her, but this is becoming an issue when she is going to school, as others are starting to tease her. Her parents have tried several things to encourage her to leave them at home but with no success. A Behavioural Therapist suggests introducing some other more appropriate items that Jane can carry - such as a second bag, both bags having to be carried (i.e. not back packs). The parents reinforce each bag being carried one at a time to start with, for a few minutes at a time, building up the length of time. Then carrying both bags at once is reinforced. When Jane goes to school now, she finds she can not carry her soft toys with both bags, but appears happy to have her hands full - with having the two bags to carry.

EXTINCTION

Extinction can be an effective way for reducing and even stopping an unwanted behaviour from being emitted. Extinction, as explained earlier in this book, is based on the cessation, ending, of the response/s that has in the past reinforced the behaviour in question. For example, if your boss suddenly stopped paying you a wage for your work, and this was the reinforcer (the pay) that encouraged you to repeat the behaviour (your weeks work) again in the future, this would be placing your work behaviour on *extinction*. It is likely you would quickly stop the behaviour, working that is, and go and do something for another company. It is of course possible you may in fact just work harder and faster, hoping that this would see your Boss start paying you again. This would be termed an *extinction burst*.

The possible dangers of using extinction are:

- **A new behaviour develops** that is more dangerous or stigmatising than the one that is being targeted for reduction. In the example used earlier, it may be that as you no longer get paid for your work, you now start stealing company property and selling it for money. The money you obtain from doing this would in turn reinforce the stealing behaviour.

- **Aggression.** Again, with the example above, it may be that you are so frustrated that you no longer get the response you used to that you are physically aggressive to your employer. Aggression is a real possibility in using extinction based strategies and if extinction is used you must guard against this possibility, and take the safety of the person and those around them into account as much as possible.

ALTERNATIVE BEHAVIOUR

Introducing an alternative behaviour is a recommended option in reducing an unwanted behaviour. Not using reinforcement to establish that new wanted behaviour is often where people go wrong, in that they don't reinforce the new wanted alternative behaviour, and just 'hope' that the person starts emitting that behaviour by luck (as you will know by now, this *isn't* how behaviour works).

Let's take a very basic example. A young child who does not like wearing her winter coats and so has a tantrum when the parents try to insist she does wear a coat before she goes outside. This can have the opposite effect of what was initially wanted, that is, the child soon associates the wearing of winter coats with grumpy faces, raised voices, even a physical struggle - and does more to try and avoid the wearing of the coat. If the parents initially reinforced the wearing of the coat (after of course establishing what the function of her behaviour (tantrums) was - in that it was just a general dislike of the look and feel of the coat, and so was tantruming in avoidance of wearing it), using a desensitising strategy, they are likely to have succeeded. For example, just having the coat in her room results in Mum and dad saying *"You are so good keeping your coat in your room, well done!"* Then after this is established, have the child carry the coat from one end of the house to the other - *"Great, good job - have 10 minutes on the PlayStation for such a good job".* This of course can be progressed a step at a time: Carrying the coat outside and back, putting the coat on inside, wearing it on the back step, back lawn, in the car, etc. Though it can be a fairly long process, long term success is very likely.

Though the above example does not really relate directly to the introduction of an alternative behaviour in its real sense, it does use the same principles. Select a behaviour that is wanted (acceptable) that can replace the unwanted behaviour. Reinforce small steps at a time until the alternative behaviour is in place, cease responding to the old unwanted behaviour when or if it still presents. **That's right - you are using extinction, but hand-in-hand with a new behaviour being introduced.**

Some examples of alternative behaviours are:

- **Constant Screaming** = New communication method introduced (*visuals, sign language/gestures, a clap*)
- **Self Injurious Behaviour** (self harm - pinching self hard) = *Tactile object to hold and interact with, koosh balls to squeeze, etc.*
- **Eating Unhealthy Snacks** (Candy and Chocolate) = Unhealthy snacks removed, *healthier snacks (muesli bars, fruit) introduced*

INCOMPATIBLE BEHAVIOUR

An incompatible behaviour can be introduced to prevent or reduce an unwanted behaviour from being emitted. Incompatible behaviours are particularly useful when a person has a disability of such a degree that makes introducing alternative behaviours difficult.

An incompatible behaviour is a behaviour that if being emitted, makes it impossible for the other unwanted behaviour to occur at the same time. For example, take a student who disrupts the class by interfering with other students work whenever he has finished his work. If a specific time consuming tactile task was introduced that he can work on when he finishes his work, he will not be able to disrupt the class. In other words, he now has a task he must concentrate on and use his hands to complete, meaning he can not go around to other students and disrupt them.

Again reinforcement of the incompatible behaviour will be needed if the person the strategy is aimed at is to emit that behaviour in the future.

TEACHING WANTED BEHAVIOURS

New Behaviours *CAN* Be Taught

I have been constantly surprised and saddened by the number of adults within disability organisations that do not know how to do even the most basic skills. Skills such as tying a shoe lace, buttoning or sometimes even zipping a jacket, and even making a cup of tea or coffee have never been taught to them.

This is a sad indictment on the organisations themselves, because people with even a severe level of intellectual disability can usually be taught these skills and others by using some fairly basic techniques. The techniques we will look at below can be used to teach these very skills to people with an intellectual disability, autism, young children, or those going through rehabilitation from brain injury.

Chaining

Chaining, or behaviour chains, is one of the more simple methods of teaching basic behaviours. Chaining refers to a set of small steps, or tasks, that are required in a specified skill. That is, a new behaviour can be broken down into other step-by-step behaviours that can be learned easier than by trying to learn the entire new behaviour at once.

The first step in designing a chaining strategy is to establish the steps needed to perform the identified behaviour for teaching. This process is usually referred to as a **Task Analysis**.

To do a task analysis, you either need to perform the behaviour yourself, noting every step, or carefully observe someone else emitting that behaviour. Though this may seem like a straight forward easy process to do, you may be surprised at how many steps are required even with a basic task. Let's look at an analysis of pouring a glass of milk as an example. The first break down takes into account the person has some basic understanding of opening cupboards and bottles, etc. The second break down considers that the person to be taught has little to no understanding of this, or associated tasks.

Example of task analysis for someone with some basic understanding

Locate cupboard with glasses

Select a glass

Place glass bottom down on kitchen bench

Locate fridge

Open fridge

Locate milk bottle

Remove milk bottle from fridge

Remove lid from milk bottle

Pour milk into glass, until almost to the top of the glass

Place lid back on bottle

Place milk back into fridge

Close fridge door

***Example of task analysis for someone with little to no basic understanding**

Locate cupboard with glasses

Place hand on cupboard door handle, hold onto handle

Pull door towards you

Stop pulling when door is open

Release handle

Look for glass

Place hand on glass

Lift glass up

Place glass on bench with open end facing up

Locate fridge

Place hand on fridge door handle, hold onto handle

Pull door towards you

Stop pulling when door is open

Release handle

Look for milk bottle

Place hand on milk bottle

Lift milk bottle up and out of fridge

Put one hand on lid of bottle

Turn lid anti-clockwise while holding bottle with other hand

When lid comes off, place lid on bench

Hold open end of bottle over glass

Tip bottle on angle so milk pours into glass

Tip bottle back to straight up when glass is almost full

Pick up lid

Place lid on bottle and turn clockwise

Place milk back in fridge

Push fridge door shut

*As you may have surmised by now, though the above example is fairly detailed, many of the 'steps' themselves could be broken down into further steps to achieve each of them. For example, how to hold a door handle, holding and turning a lid, tipping a bottle to pour, etc. To teach some of these steps may also require hand-over-hand prompting (as discussed in more detail later in this chapter). Depending on the level of understanding of the person you are working with, determining the amount of steps and how much they need to be broken down will vary. Teaching a wanted behaviour to a child or adult with a severe intellectual disability or autism would require smaller steps (and subsequently more steps) than if teaching a new behaviour to someone who was typically developed.

TASK ANALYSIS EXAMPLES

Brushing Teeth	Tying shoes
Pick up the tooth brush Wet the brush *Take the cap off the tube* Put paste on the brush *Brush the outside of the bottom row of teeth* Brush the outside of the top row of teeth *Brush the biting surface of the top row of teeth* Brush the biting surface of the bottom row of teeth *Try to make yourself understood while answering the question of someone outside the door* Brush the inside surface of the bottom row of teeth *Brush the inside surface of the top row of teeth* Spit *Rinse the brush* Replace the brush in the holder *Grasp cup* Fill cup with water *Rinse teeth with*	*(shorter version for kids who need help with the first few steps)* Grab one lace in each hand. Pull the shoe laces tight with a vertical pull. Cross the shoe laces. Pull the front lace around the back of the other. Put that lace through the hole. Tighten the laces with a horizontal pull. Make a bow. Tighten the bow Tying shoes (longer version) Pinch the laces. Pull the laces. Hang the ends of the laces from the corresponding sides of the shoe. Pick up the laces in the corresponding hands. Lift the laces above the shoe. Cross the right lace over the left one to form a tepee. Bring the left lace toward the student. Pull the left lace through the tepee. Pull the laces away from one another. Bend the left lace to form a loop. Pinch the loop with the left hand. Bring the right lace over the

water Spit *Replace cup in holder* Wipe mouth on towel *Screw cap back on tube*	fingers and around the loop. Push the right lace through the hole. Pull the loops away from one another.
Doing Homework Unpack schoolbag Retrieve Homework book Get pen and paper from bag Place all items on desk Read homework tasks Write answers to tasks on paper Show parents for checking Place homework book, paper and pen back in schoolbag	**Taking a "Sickie" From Work** *(Humorous)* Phone boss 5 minutes before start time Practice coughing while phone rings Mutter, in low tone, "Can't, *(cough)* work, sick *(splutter)* today" Listen to, but take no notice of, what boss says in reply Cough again, moan as if in great pain, sob a little Mutter *"Wanted to work so much, (cough), but so sick, can't come (scream out in pain) in to work - can't walk (splutter, cough, moan)"* Listen to boss's reply again, take some notice Now, hang up and dial correct number and repeat!

Forward Chaining

After your task analysis is complete, and recorded in written steps, you now need to begin teaching each step!

There are two main ways to use chaining, one is **forward chaining**, and the other is **backward chaining**.

With forward chaining, the steps are taught in the order they take place. For example, with pouring a glass of milk as above, the first step to be taught is locating the correct cupboard. So, the teacher would prompt (verbally, or physically guide) the student to the correct cupboard, **then the teacher would do the rest of the steps.** When the student (person learning the new behaviour) can locate the cupboard by walking to it unprompted, the teacher would then teach the next step (place hand on cupboard door handle, hold onto handle) again by way of prompting and/or modeling the correct behaviour (modeling is also covered later in this chapter), then, again, the teacher does the rest of the steps. So at this stage the student now does the first two steps and the teacher does the others. This continues systematically until eventually the student does all the steps unprompted and so has now learnt this new wanted behaviour.

Reinforcing each step that the person performs correctly is of course vitally important; remember the basics of behaviour? Reinforcement supplied immediately after a behaviour is emitted, increases the likelihood that behaviour will be repeated in the future.

Backward Chaining

Backward chaining is simply the reverse of forward chaining, that is, instead of the person learning the new behaviour doing the first step first, then the next, etc, they firstly do the last step, then the second to last and last step, and so on.

For example, in the example above the teacher would do all the steps up until pushing the fridge door shut, which is what the 'student' does (with prompting as required, and of course *reinforcement once the correct behaviour is emitted).*

When should you use either forward or backward chaining?

Results from research on comparing forward chaining and backward chaining has shown that both are equally effective, though there may be, according to some studies, a slight advantage in using a backward chaining strategy in some situations, particularly when teaching a sport related behaviour.

Our advice is to make a decision on which one to try based on your knowledge of the person who is to be taught the wanted behaviour. That is, if they are highly motivated by the end result of the behaviour (getting a cookie from the fridge), which is also the positive reinforcer, use backward chaining. This is because that last step also means instant access to the reinforcer, increasing the likelihood of that step being repeated in the future. Once this last step is mastered, they now also perform the second to last step, and being able to go straight to the last step that has the reinforcer will reinforce this second to last step. If the wanted behaviour being taught is a behaviour where the end result is not necessarily as clearly reinforcing to the person (for example, getting paper to rip from a box, instead of ripping own clothes) try the forward chaining approach. Remember that no matter which approach you take, each step needs to be reinforced to increase the likelihood it will be repeated.

The way each step is taught should look like the following (showing first step only):

Forward Chaining

Prompt or model step

|

Step Performed

|

Step reinforced

|

Next steps performed by teacher/support person

|

Return to first step of process (prompt until that step is mastered (no longer prompt reliant)

|

Prompt or model step (or let person perform this step if they can at this stage)

|

Step Performed

|

Step reinforced

Backward Chaining

All but last step performed by teacher/support person

|

Prompt or model last step

|

Step Performed

|

Step reinforced

|

All but last step that is mastered (no longer prompt reliant) is performed by teacher

|

Prompt or model step

I

Step Performed

I

Step reinforced

Continue this process until the student is performing all steps of the behaviour without prompts. It may be they may always require some support for certain parts of the behaviour process, but this is ok.

MODELING AND PROMPTING

Modeling Appropriate Behaviour

Whether the task at hand is to model all the steps of a wanted behaviour, or to model one step at a time (as in chaining strategies), we need to ensure certain factors are taken into account.

Exactly what is 'modeling appropriate behaviour'? Modeling refers to demonstrating to or showing the person to be taught the behaviour, exactly what that behaviour looks like, sounds like, in some cases even feels like. For example, if the wanted behaviour is to take a dirty plate from the table, empty the scraps in the bin, rinse it and then place it in the dishwasher, that is what you do slowly and clearly while the person to be taught watches you. In some cases you would prompt them to observe what you were doing, get them to walk alongside you as you go to the bin with the plate so they can see exactly how you scrape the leftovers into the bin, then how to rinse the plate properly, and the correct placement in the dishwasher.

If teaching manners, you would ensure you slowly and clearly use the words *"thank you"* and *"please"* in the appropriate places of a conversation you have with someone, as the person to be taught listens.

With a behaviour such as combing hair, you again would show the correct movements, but may also model the behaviour on the person combing their hair so they can feel the sensation of how hard the comb should be pressed to their head. Remember, though this all seems obvious and easy to most people, to some it is a totally new experience, and they may struggle to comprehend the amount of force to be used if they have not emitted that behaviour themselves before.

Basic Principles of Modeling a Wanted Behaviour

- **Don't overwhelm the person with too many steps at once:** Imagine if someone was showing you how to operate a control panel of a nuclear power plant, though they may show you slowly and clearly - if they went through all 200 or so procedures at once, you would very quickly forget the vast majority of what they did. Instead, if it is a complex task (or a task involving many different steps), model just one or two steps at a time. If using forward chaining, you would firstly model the step the person was up to trying themselves before they attempted it, not model all the steps and then ask them to do just one. Backward chaining, you would go through all the steps, then make sure the last step (or the one the person is up to next) was demonstrated extra clearly and as slow as needed according the level of ability of the person being taught.

- **Talk or sign the person through the behaviour:** Talk, sign (or use whatever communication the person understands) as you model the behaviour to assist in the understanding of the steps. For example *"Now I take the plate carefully to the bin, making sure I don't drop anything on the way ..."*. Remember you may need to 'fade' the communicating through the behaviour if you need to show the behaviour many times, as you do not want the person also talking through the behaviour each time they emit it in future.

- **Consistency:** As highlighted many times through this book, **consistency is extremely important** if you want to succeed in teaching a new behaviour, or reducing an unwanted behaviour. If the correct way to walk down the corridor is to keep to the far left, then that is what you should model each and every time you demonstrate the behaviour to the person being taught. If nine times out of ten you stay on the left, and once you walk down the middle, you have now shown that you don't *really* have to stick to the left. You also need others who support the person following the same steps in the same order, or once again you are creating confusion to the person. Is the correct way following steps 1, 2, and 3, or is it following steps 2, 1, and 3?

- **Have A Plan**: Know the behaviour perfectly yourself before you start trying to model the appropriate behaviour to the person being taught. Imagine if you went to have your first driving lesson and the person teaching you wasn't sure how to do up the seatbelts, or didn't know where the indicator lever was, you would hardly be filled with confidence. What would be more concerning is that because the person teaching you does not seem to find putting a seat-belt on an important step, you would follow that same behaviour yourself - possibly with disastrous consequences. Practice the behaviour by yourself first, or at the very least, think through all the correct steps before demonstrating them so you show confidence and show the correct steps in the correct order.

Prompting

Prompts are cues or guides given by a teacher, parent or support person to aid another persons understanding about emitting a certain behaviour at a certain time.

Prompts can be audible (sound) (e.g. verbal prompts, electronic sounds, or other), physical (e.g. by hand, tactile stimulation, or other) or visual (e.g. coloured light, picture card, or other). The type of prompt to be used will depend on the person being taught, the teacher, and environmental factors. See the table below for some examples:

Audible Prompts	Verbal - *"Step Forward"*
	Electronic Sound - *Pedestrian Crossing Buzzer*
	Other Sounds - *Clicking fingers for attention to task*
Physical Prompts	Hand Over Hand - *guiding the students hand as they learn to write*
	Tactile Stimulation - *Textured surface on hand rail when end of walkway is near*
	Other - *Raised tread on ground near crossings to alert people with visual impairment* (another type of tactile prompt)
Visual Prompts	Pictures/Posters - *Red Light Picture - Prompt for stop when angry*
	Picture Communication Card - *Hand over picture card of drink to remind student of time to drink.*
	Electronic Lights - *Pedestrian Crossing, green man and red man.*

Prompts are an important part of a behavioural strategy when teaching a new behaviour. **The fading of prompts is also important if the person is to learn to emit the behaviour without becoming prompt-reliant.** That is, if you are teaching safe road crossing skills, and you prompt the student when they must stop, when to look, and when to cross, you need to *slowly remove your prompts as the student becomes competent in the behaviour.* If you don't, the student may not emit the appropriate road crossing behaviour unless they hear (or see) your prompts each time they are in a road crossing situation.

Generalisation of Prompts and of Behaviour

When teaching a new behaviour, where possible you should have other people who are involved in the person's life follow through with the strategy you are using. That is, if teaching road crossing skills have others on some occasions give the prompts for stop, look, listen, and cross as well as yourself giving those prompts on other occasions.

Use differing environments; do not always use the same environment or situation. This is particularly important as the person progresses with their learning. When first teaching the new behaviour/s you may need to use the same environment on the first few occasions to build a basic understanding, but then ensure you vary the location, vary the person giving the prompts, and other factors.

A common issue this author has come across is where self-proclaimed experts of teaching children with autism play skills and verbal skills, can demonstrate to the Parent that the child can identify the ball, how to interact with it, and even use appropriate speech such as "hello" "please" and "Thank you". What they do not realise is that the child only identifies a certain colour and/or size ball as a ball, and only uses those words when with that specific teacher. Sometimes Parents or others mistake this for the child simply being stubborn or 'naughty', when in fact it is because the teacher never generalised the behaviour to other people, other similar objects, other environments and even different times of day.

BEHAVIOURAL MOMENTUM

As parents/support people, we know there are some behaviours that a child will demonstrate with little or no fuss. For example, getting the ice-cream out for desert, making themselves a chocolate drink, playing with their toys (these are all 'preferred behaviours'). ***This strategy uses the 'momentum' of a preferred behaviour (or task) to carry across to a behaviour the child may not wish to emit.*** (Note that this strategy is not for teaching a wanted behaviour that the person does not yet know how to emit, but more-so to have the person emit a behaviour that they know, but are usually unwilling to emit).

Below is a list of the steps you can follow to use this approach.

1) **List the tasks that your child will perform (behaviours they will emit) with little to no fuss.** Also list the behaviours that you can not get the child to emit without a Behavioural Incident usually occurring.

2) **Tell your child you are going to play a game.** *"I am going to get you to do some tasks for me and see how good you are doing them"*. Before you receive the 'this is just a trick, I don't want to do any jobs' type response, quickly ask them to do one of the preferred behaviours. E.g. *"Bring me the ice-cream please"*. *"Now a plate and a spoon"*. Verbally praise your child for each task they perform

without fuss. Now give them a small helping of ice-cream (or whatever the preferred task related to – for example, picking up a fun toy – playing with the toy, or bringing a book – reading some of the book to them, etc).

3) **Now ask one more preferred behaviour to be demonstrated.** Again praise and reward the child.

4) **Now, ask for a non-preferred behaviour to be emitted** (but ensure it is not a huge one to start with, again start small). E.g. *"You are doing great; now please take your dirty clothes to the laundry"*.

5) **Continue this process, intermingle the preferred with the non-preferred behaviour requests.** Repeat this process over four or five sessions; eventually you should notice improvement when requesting the once non-preferred behaviours to be performed at standard times (not within the behaviour momentum sessions).

Remember to **always praise the child each time they perform a task.** *"Well done, you did a great job!"*

RESPONSE COST

This strategy is for reducing unwanted behaviours that are emitted at a high rate. That is, the unwanted behaviour is seen many times in a short period of time and you want to reduce this down to a low amount, if not eventually have it stop altogether.

(Note that although we use the term 'child' this strategy can also be used for adults with an intellectual disability, autism, or other disability).

1. If your child receives pocket money, tell them how you would like to give them a little more than what they usually get. For example, let's say they get $5 a fortnight; you may like to tell them you will now give them $7.00 a fortnight, if they have a token left on the chart at the agreed finish time (as explained in the next steps). Alternatively (as not all children get pocket money, or you may not wish to use money as a reinforcer), you can ask them what special treat they would like to get. Maybe a trip to the movies, or a special dinner? Either way, agree what it is.

2. Now set up a chart with say five tokens (though this number will be higher if the unwanted behaviour you wish to reduce is very frequent – see example in the table for an explanation of how to decide on the number of tokens to begin with). Set them a target day/time for when they will receive the special reward (agreed in step one), as well as establishing when the time period starts from. To start with, make this target day or time quite close. The first time

you use the token chart, you may set the finish target time only one or two hours away (especially if the behaviour is very frequent, and you would normally expect to see that behaviour in that time period). You want them to be successful the first time at least, so they can see what you are asking is achievable, and so they get to experience receiving the reinforcement. Explain that if they display the *unwanted* behaviour in that time, you will **remove one token each time they emit the behaviour**. If you are using an increase in pocket money, they receive that extra money as long as they have **at least one token left on the chart at the agreed finish time**. If using a specific item or special treat as the reinforcer, explain that they will lose one token each time they display the behaviour, **but as long as at least one token is left at the set finish time, they get the treat (reinforcement).**

3. Once they have shown a general decrease in the amount of times the unwanted behaviour is being emitted, in other words they are receiving the reinforcement in each time period, slowly decrease the number of tokens they can lose before missing out on that special treat. You can also slowly increase the time period that the tokens may be removed in. I.e., they may have to go three days with only four tokens, that is - three opportunities to emit the unwanted behaviour before losing their last token and subsequently the reinforcer. Obviously, you are now (hopefully) getting a gradual decline in the frequency of the Behavioural Incidents, and eventually may see them end altogether.

In the table below you will read an example of how this strategy can be set up, and how it works, and the possible results.

Day One	You have observed that Jonathon stamps his feet and shouts on average ten times a day
Day Two	As Jonathon emits this unwanted behaviour on average <u>ten</u> times per day, you set up a chart with <u>eleven</u> tokens on it. This is because you want Jonathon to succeed the first couple of days, so he gets to experience the reinforcement if he still has at least one token left on the chart at 6pm each day.
Day Three	Your first day of using the token chart has started. Each time Jonathon stamps his feet and shouts, you remove one token. At 6pm, Jonathon still has one or two tokens still on the chart. You tell Jonathon *"Well done Jonathon, you still have tokens on the chart, you get an extra ten minutes computer time tonight."* (this is his preferred reinforcement).
Day Four	The same results as Day Three are achieved.
Day Five	Today, you start the token chart with just ten tokens. This means that Jonathon can only emit the behaviour a maximum of nine times

	today if he is to be left with at least one token, and receive his preferred reinforcement.
Day Six	Jonathon unfortunately failed to have at least one token left yesterday, and so missed out on his reinforcement. So you again start with ten tokens.
Day Seven	Jonathon succeeded yesterday in having one token left on his chart, and so received his extra computer time.
Day Eight	Again Jonathon received his reinforcement by having at least one token left yesterday, so today you start the chart with nine tokens. This means Jonathon can now only emit the unwanted behaviour a maximum of eight times and still receive his preferred reinforcement.
Day Nine	Continue with nine tokens, Jonathon is getting success each day.
Day Ten	Now reducing to six tokens, meaning a maximum of five times Jonathon can emit the unwanted behaviour before he does not receive the preferred reinforcement.

In the example on the last pages, the strategy would continue following the same process until only two or three tokens are on the chart each morning, and after some time Jonathon does not emit the unwanted behaviour more than only once or twice per week – a huge improvement on originally around 70 times per week.

Important Notes on Response Cost

Understanding the Strategy: The child or adult does not necessarily need to understand exactly how the strategy works. That is, if the person is severely intellectually disabled and does not understand an explanation that would be required to explain how the tokens work, this does not matter. The person will learn from the basics of how behaviour works, that is, when they have emitted the unwanted behaviour less, they get something they like, when they have emitted the unwanted behaviour the same amount of times they used to, they don't receive it. Reduce the number of starting tokens slowly, because if you jump to a very low number quickly the person may simply struggle too much to reduce the number of unwanted behaviours, and so give up even trying.

If You Have Setbacks – Don't Panic: If you find the person is going through all the tokens in each time period, simply increase the starting amount of tokens or shorten the time period. Remember, **the person must have some success, if they are to want to repeat the lower frequency of unwanted behaviours again.**

Varying The Reinforcement: Satiation may become a problem if the person is getting the same reinforcement every time. Satiation refers to when a person has received a reinforcement so many times that it is no longer anything special. Imagine if chocolate was your most loved reinforcement (as it is for many of us). Suddenly though, you have access to as much chocolate as you want, yet your partner is attempting to entice you into giving him/her a back rub in return for them going out and getting you a box of chocolates. You are not going to be the slightest bit encouraged, seeing you already have all the chocolate you want. So, with this strategy you may need to have a few known preferred reinforcements you can use and vary them from day to day.

You can of course also use other behavioural strategies, such as introducing alternative behaviours so the person can learn more appropriate ways of getting the response they require. Whether that is attention, to be allowed to go to their room because it's too noisy, etc. Also, keep in mind the other basics you have learnt. Every behaviour has a function, there must be something reinforcing the unwanted behaviour, so what is it? Again, be consistent, and ensure others are following the Response Cost strategy the same way you are. Also, stick to the rules (so to speak), that is, do not use it as a punishment for other unwanted behaviours. If the identified unwanted behaviour was screaming you shouldn't also remove a token because they would not eat their vegetables.

Note: Response Cost is not really a punishment based strategy, in that you are not removing something from the person, as the reinforcements they may or may not get are additional to what they normally receive.

When teaching a new (wanted) behaviour, remember:

- **Vary the teachers**
- **Vary the environment**
- **Vary the time of day and vary the day**
- **If teaching recognition or use of an object, vary the object colour and style (where applicable)**
- **Fade the use of prompts once the behaviour is being emitted as required**
- **Provide positive reinforcement for correct responses**
- **Fade reinforcement as the teaching progresses**
- **Ensure the behaviour is maintained over time, by using random reinforcement in future days/weeks**
- **Ensure others in the environment model the wanted behaviour appropriately**

When reducing an unwanted behaviour, remember:

- Ignore the unwanted behaviour, but reinforce the wanted behaviour

- Introduce an alternative or incompatible behaviour

- Remember, all behaviour has a function to the person emitting that behaviour. Find out what the function is, and provide another way for the person to communicate the problem

PREVENTING A CRISIS

Much focus goes into what people can do in a crisis, yet often little focus goes on what people can do to avoid the crisis from occurring to start with. This chapter will give you some basic information that will help you to prevent a crisis that has resulted from a person's unwanted behaviour.

Preventing a behavioural crisis (a situation where a person's behaviour is a danger to themselves or others) comes down to three main factors:

1) Recognising early warning signs

2) Acting early

3) Providing appropriate support

Recognising early warning signs
Everyone emits certain behaviours that are specific to them in that they usually occur immediately before they emit behaviour that is either frightening, inappropriate (shouting, swearing in anger) or harmful to them or others (What we term as unwanted behaviours). These behaviours, which we will term *'Early Warning Signs'*, are often unique to that person, in other words not everyone will show the same 'signs' before a behavioural crisis as others show. So, the first piece of advice about preventing a crisis is:

Learn the specific early warning signs (EWS) for the people you support

Some of these EWS may be tapping their fingers, their face becoming 'flushed', a sad or angry facial expression, etc.

Though everyone will often emit behaviour unique to them before an incident of aggression or other unwanted behaviour, there are some guidelines about recognising when a person needs some support to help prevent their behaviour escalating to what I term *'the point of no return'*. This is the point where no matter what people say or do, it is unlikely to have any real effect on the persons behaviour, and we can do little but 'let them vent' and keep ourselves and others safe.

Anxiety

Anxiety is a good descriptive term for the EWS behaviours that you will notice leading up to a behavioural crisis.

Some of the more common signs of anxiety are: pacing back and forth, wringing hands together, a raised voice, withdrawing from communicating, muttering, rocking back and forth at a fast or intense rate. In fact, as a general rule we can say that *any increase or change from normal behaviour may be a sign that the person is anxious*, and that they may be headed for emitting behaviour that may be harmful to them or to others.

What You Can Do

Firstly, you need to **ACT EARLY**.

The longer you let the person become more and more anxious, the harder it will be to prevent a crisis situation developing.

You need to find out **WHAT IS WRONG, AND OFFER TO HELP**

Explain to the person that it appears something is upsetting or worrying them, and **ask them if they would they like to tell you what it is?** If the person does not have good communication skills (or may even be non-verbal and unskilled in sign language), **offer an activity that you know the person usually enjoys**. This will act as a redirection, and may help them refocus their mind from what it is that is upsetting or worrying them.

If the person does tell you what it is that is upsetting them, **be empathetic**, that is, explain how you can understand that must be upsetting or concerning for them, and you can see now why they would be feeling anxious about it (remember to use terminology they will understand). Again, offer an activity that you know they enjoy, maybe having a cold or warm drink, going for a walk, listening to some music, having a snack, etc. **Spend time with them so they can talk to you more about what happened**. Catharsis (release of emotions or bad feelings) is a good way of easing anxiety.

Be Supportive but be Safe

You may not know exactly how anxious the person really is at the stage you enquire what is wrong.

Speak in a way that is supportive rather than confrontational. Ensure your tone of voice is neutral, in other words, it doesn't sound angry nor demanding, neither does it sound condescending or disrespectful. Ask questions that invite a descriptive answer, rather than just a yes or no. For example, don't ask *"Are you feeling sad?"* do ask *"What is making you feel sad?"*

Be a good listener, give them time to reply, and don't 'butt in', let them speak. Also, listen for what the real message is that they may be trying to tell you. For example, someone who tells you *"I'm not sad about anything, I had a great morning out, and I don't care if I missed Mum's phone call!"* The real message here seems to be that they *"missed mums phone call"*. The best response would probably be: *"Oh no, you missed your Mum's call, I know how you usually really enjoy hearing from her. Here, let me see if I can arrange for you to give her a call now."*

Because you are entering into the 'unknown' sometimes when going to support a person who is showing signs of anxiety, **you need to be thinking about your own personal safety at this time.**

There are some basics around safety that you should follow; these are highlighted below:

Keeping Safe

- **ALWAYS STAND AT LEAST ONE LEG LENGTH AWAY FROM THE PERSON.** This way, if they are more anxious than you realised and react physically to you asking what the problem is, you can avoid a sudden punch or kick in your direction. *This safe distance also ensures you do not invade that person's personal space, because if you do you may make them feel more anxious and elevate their behaviour.*

- **STAND FACING TOWARDS YOUR SAFEST EXIT ROUTE.** If the person does react physically towards you, don't stand around and wait to be hit, move straight towards that exit, and keep moving. Once you are a safe distance away you can call for help, or at least take up a position where you can safely observe what the person is doing, and also give them space to calm down. *(If the exit point is directly behind you, obviously you can not stand with your back facing the person. Instead, stand on an angle allowing ease of escape if needed)*

- **HAVE A PLAN.** Before you approach the person to see what is wrong, have a plan in your own head of what to do should they respond physically. Know where you can exit the location, where and who you can seek help from, and who else may need to be assisted to leave the immediate area if the situation worsens.

Team Work and Consistency

When someone is anxious and becoming agitated, supporting them so you can prevent a crisis can be both tiring and stressful. *If you have another person to help you in this process, when possible, let them take over the support if the process is continuing for a long period of time.* If you get tired and stressed, you will quickly become less patient and less tolerant and may end up losing your cool and possibly worsening the situation. The person may very well become more anxious, and end up hitting out at you or emitting other behaviour that hurts someone or damages property.

If you need your partner or team-mate to take over the support, ensure there is a consistent approach. That new support person needs to follow the same principles that you have been following, firm but calm, listen to what they have to say, maintain a safe distance from the person, know the exit point.

The Next Step, if the Situation Worsens

If the person's behaviour does not change, and they still show signs of anxiety, and in fact the behaviours shown seem to indicate an elevation is occurring towards behaviour that may become harmful, you need to take a different approach.

You now need to start being more directive with the person. Give choices about what you want the person to do. For example *"I need you to either move to your room where you will not upset others, or I need you to move outside and walk off what is making you upset".* Stick to the choices given, and once given to the person wait a while. If no response, repeat the same choices again. If the person challenges you, and questions why you can tell them what to do, explain it isn't about you, you need them to decide on the choices given. **Do not argue or discuss who is in charge, rather – stick to the original directions.**

If still no change and the person continues to escalate in regards to the behaviour emitted, it is now best to remove yourself and others from the immediate environment. **Give the person space to 'let off steam', until they have worked through the energy that they obviously have that was created from what it was that upset them, they will be a potential risk to themselves and others.** However, remain in a location where you can keep an eye on them, or at least listen out to make sure they do not harm themselves (purposely or accidentally). Like a pressure cooker, if you try and block the one vent for the steam to escape (or for the person to get that 'bad energy' out of them) an explosion will occur.

If the person's behaviour escalates to a stage where you believe someone is at imminent risk of getting hurt, seek professional input either from a mental health crisis team, or the Police.

INTELLECTUAL DISABILITY

The strategies outlined in this book are mostly also suitable for children, and adults with an intellectual disability. Below is some information about intellectual disability, and its impact on the strategies and information supplied in this book.

Having an Intellectual disability is partly a battle with understanding the World to the degree that others without an intellectual disability do, and partly battling society's views of people with an intellectual disability.

So what is an Intellectual Disability?

Intellectual Disability goes by other names, depending on which country you live in. In the USA the term **Mentally Retarded** or **Mentally Disabled** is still used. In the United Kingdom **Learning Disability** is the description given to this disability. What these names mean is the person has received this diagnosis according to set criteria used in measurement or assessment procedures that have been used by a Clinical Psychologist, Psychiatrist, or other person registered to administer psychometric tests. The most common criteria used is that the persons IQ (Intelligence Quotient) is below 70 to 75 (depending on the specific criteria used), **and** the person has difficulties in two of ten specific adaptive skills, such as communication, daily living, using transport, school work, etc. There is also a third criterion which states that these difficulties were present before they reached the age of 18 years (again, some criteria use a different age, but almost always this falls between 16 and 18).

Different categories are then used to identify where that individual is placed in the degree to which the intellectual disability affects them. The original categories, though now rarely used, were profound, severe, moderate, and mild. The more common categories used now are based on the level of need the person has for support. This may be 'needs full support with all aspects of daily life', or that they just need 'occasional support'.

People with an intellectual disability are limited by our attitude towards them
Possibly the best approach to how you will support a person with an intellectual disability, is to *look at what they can do*, rather than what they can't, then grow these abilities to outweigh any challenges they face. Let's look at an example to highlight this approach. Let's say Bob struggles with communicating with others, verbally as well as using signs and gestures. This in turn has isolated Bob from most people, as many see no reason to try and get to know him as he appears to make no attempt to try and communicate in return. However, Bob is very good at art. He can paint and sketch very well. His support person concentrates on encouraging Bob to use this skill, and soon Bob is turning out up to a dozen beautiful pieces of art each week, and enjoying it. His Support Person places some of Bob's artwork in a local art gallery (with Bob' permission), and soon people are traveling from all over the city to see Bob's work.

Many of the fans of Bob's artwork not only want to purchase it, providing a source of income for him, but also want to meet the artist. Soon Bob makes regular appearances each month at the art gallery to meet those who enjoy his work. Bob is now appreciated for the skills he has, rather than shunned for what he struggles to do well.

Sometimes, particularly with a child or adult greatly affected by the level of their disability, it is difficult to see what skills they do have, as their challenges seem overwhelming. But everyone has something they do well, even if that is only their presence that brings happiness – this in itself can be a huge gift to others.

People with an intellectual disability are also often restricted to only being functional with limited activities, because they have never been given exposure to the full range of activities that others have. How can they learn those skills, if people do not let them try because "*They have a disability – and so won't be able to do it*"? In my career I have also often heard the term "*Don't set them up to fail*", in other words, they don't want to give them the opportunity to try something, just in case they can't do it to the same level others can. I particularly despise that approach, it is very limiting and disrespectful of people's goals and ambitions, and it can only do harm and highlights the ignorance of people who have little understanding of people with disabilities.

Focus on dreams and goals, forget the 'can't dos'
If a person with an intellectual disability and severe physical disability has a goal to be an astronaut, who are we to tell them that their goal is nonsense and their dream is just a waste of time and they should just forget it. Without our dreams and hopes, we have nothing. Instead of the "*can't do that, because you are disabled*" approach,

you should be saying "*Great! Wouldn't that be exciting and amazing to be an astronaut, what a cool goal!*" Now, **focus on that goal, break the goal down into small steps.** What do you need to do to be an astronaut? Firstly, you need to be able to read basic words so you can understand the control panel; you also need to know the basics about space and space travel. So, the person's current goals become:

> 1) Learning how to read twelve basic words used on a control panel (On, off, open, close, etc).
>
> 2) Reading, or having read to them, books about space, space travel, looking at star maps, pictures of planets, rockets, space shuttles, etc.

You have now given the person huge motivation to work on advancing their skills by way of achievable goals, without taking their dream away from them. If the goals are not met within the time period envisaged, you can either increase the time period (If they have made some progress), or re-evaluate what the goals are, and how the support is being provided.

Once goals are achieved, set the next goals as further steps towards the person's ultimate goal. They may not ever get to be an astronaut, but they will live a happy and rewarding life striving to get as close to that dream as they possibly can, and enjoying the knowledge and skills they learn on the way.

Communication: Use whatever communication methods that work best. Do not just use verbal prompts because that is what we suggest, if sign language or physical gestures are what your child/adult understands, then use those. Also keep in mind that it is very common for a person with an intellectual disability to develop certain behaviours as a way of communicating something. E.g. they don't like that food, or going to that environment, or there is too much noise, so they emit a behaviour that results in them being moved somewhere else, or being given different food, etc. If they have trouble communicating in other ways, this may be the only way they can escape from what they do not like. You will need to introduce other ways they can communicate that fact, try picture cards, a certain gesture or sign language.

Picture Exchange Communication System (PECS) is a great communication tool for those who can not communicate verbally. However, they are rarely used, and certainly rarely used to their full extent. Talk with a speech and language therapist about teaching the person you support in using this tool, if the therapist seems negative towards PECS we strongly recommend you research it, and give it a try anyway. On the next page is a very brief description of how to introduce just one picture exchange.

Teaching a communication (picture exchange) request for a sandwich

I. Take a clear photo of a sandwich that you know the person prefers to eat

II. Laminate the photo in a size that is right for the person to handle

III. Pair the picture with the giving of the sandwich. That is, just before giving the person their sandwich, hand them the photo, and then take the photo back as you pass them the sandwich

IV. Do this several times over the next few meals, eventually prompt the person to hand the photo to you, before you pass them the sandwich.

V. Once they show some understanding that the photo handed over equals a sandwich in return, place the photo in an accessible place where they can get it and hand it to their support person at any time.

Of course, once you have achieved this first 'picture exchange', you can start introducing others, including requests like "want" or "don't want". Some will argue this limits some people who could potentially learn verbal commands (that is, saying the words or request), but you can and should pair the picture exchange with saying the word at the same time. So, as per the example above, when teaching the picture exchange, say the word *"sandwich"* as well as taking the picture from them. Encourage them (if applicable) to say the word as well, as they hand the picture over.

Plain language: Do not use 'jargon' or slang as this may confuse the person's understanding. Though the use of slang may be common place in your culture, the fact it does not use everyday words and terms grouped together in a standard fashion is enough to cause confusion and frustration to someone with lesser intellectual ability.

Visual Cues and Environmental Specific Cues: Where possible, show the person the actual objects, rooms, people, tasks that you are referring to, rather than just talking about them. The old saying 'a picture is worth a thousand words' is all to true in communication.

Patience and Repetition: You need extra patience when working with someone who has an intellectual disability. Keep in mind that often some behaviours are more difficult to modify than others, as the person may struggle with learning more appropriate behaviours. You may also need a high amount of repetition in what you are trying to teach. That is, if you are ignoring the inappropriate behaviour (extinction) and paying lots of attention to the appropriate behaviours, you may need to do this more than you would for a person without an intellectual disability. It is believed that some people with fetal alcohol syndrome (also affected by an intellectual disability) may need to have a specific rule or term repeated up to a thousand times before they fully comprehend what the term is about. This may seem to be a huge amount, but remember it may need be repeated only two to three times a day as the situation comes up, so across a year this is 700 to 1000 or more times, so a huge amount of energy per day is not needed. In fact, if you are sharing the support with others (teachers, partner, or family members) it may be that each individual only needs to remind the person once every day or two, to achieve the desired result.

AUTISM

What Is Autism?

Rather than supply a typical clinical description of what Autism is, and how it will affect the person diagnosed with it and their family / support people, below is the explanation of Autism that I have given to many Parents and others who asked that simple question that many have *"What is Autism, what does it mean?"* My description, or rather explanation of Autism, is from my observations, experiences from my work, discussions / assessments with those who have autism, and conversations with those people who have had their lives affected by supporting a person with autism.

Being In an Alien World *(written from the point of view of how someone with Autism may see the World, and how they would explain having autism)*

To some people with autism, the World around them is alien, in that they just don't seem to be a part of it, or maybe more rightly described, the World doesn't seem to be a home that they feel comfortable in. All the noise, motion, shapes, colours, and so many various personalities that confront a person with autism every day, all seem so over the top and just plain irritating and stressful.

Communicating with others does not just seem awkward and sometimes even unnecessary *(after all, why would I want to discuss your World with you, when it doesn't interest me in the slightest)* but it is also yet another task that makes me have to consider what someone else is feeling or thinking about. Trying to understand and accept that another person's feelings and ideas are just as important as mine is not easy. Yet sometimes when I do focus on other peoples feelings, it becomes simply overwhelming, and I find I either get very angry, sad, worried, or completely frustrated. What is in **my World**, in **my mind**, is all that I concentrate on, partially because it helps me block out an environment that is full of other meanings, emotions, ideas, that just get on top of me and make me loose my own thoughts.

My own interests though, are very important to me. I am usually happy to communicate about, or at least spend huge amounts of time interacting with, my own interests. These interests often become an obsession to me, and I would be quite happy to spend every waking moment just interacting with them. Collecting certain objects is common, and look out those who may try and interfere with my collections! However, as quickly and as strongly as these obsessions start up, they may also end, and they will hold little to no interest to me in the future.

I really do not like things to go differently from how I expected them or how I had planned out they would occur. *It pays not to go changing plans at the last moment, as it isn't just annoying, it makes me feel like I have completely lost control of what was happening to me, and I may get very upset or even angry.* Many people don't realise just how frustrating and upsetting this can be for me, and some even think I am just being 'naughty' or being a 'spoilt brat' because I didn't get my own way. You need to realise that this is not how it is, instead let me give you an example so you might understand why I get upset with sudden changes to my routine. Imagine you were going on holiday; you drive for three hours solid to get to your destination of choice, to find when you arrive in the town you expected to arrive in, somehow, you have driven in exactly the wrong direction and arrived at a completely different town. You have nowhere to stay, and you don't know anyone there to ask for help. Imagine how you feel – frightened, upset, and angry, no amount of smiles and comments of *"don't make a fuss about it"* will make you feel any better. That is how I sometimes feel when something goes very differently from what I expected.

Things are very 'black and white' to me, or putting it another way, I think very concretely, what I see and hear is what I accept as being so. So, if you use slang or jargon, instead of just being straight forward with what you tell me, I will not only get confused, but frustrated, and maybe angry too. Why use slang, when there are terms there for describing what it is you want to say or describe? It's the same with rules, I like people to follow what is expected of them, rules are there for a purpose, and people should just follow them. When I know and understand a rule, I will rarely break it, and if I do I may upset myself, and be disappointed and frustrated that I did what I so did not want to do, or want others to do. Sometimes I may even try and punish myself when I have broken a rule that I previously accepted and followed, and sometimes I may even try and punish others who I believe have broken a rule.

Words, both written and verbal, are ok – but pictures and objects hold a lot more meaning. They are concrete – what I see is what is real, what is actual, where words are just that – words, and are somewhat abstract, no matter how well they are put to me. If I am struggling to understand something, try explaining it to me with the use of photos, drawings, or icons – it may help quite a bit in getting me to understand. Lastly, I ask you to get to know me over a long period of time, I struggle to get to know people and to like people – after all, you will never understand exactly how I see the World, just like I may never understand how you see it. So again, give me time, be patient, I am really a neat person, I just see things different from you that's all.

Below, I have listed some factors you need to keep in mind when using the strategies as outlined in this book when supporting someone with autism.

Concrete Thinking: If it is black and white, it is black and white – not white and black. This type of thinking is common in autism. Because of this we need to ensure all our requests are made using plain language, no slang terms or abbreviated language. Saying to a typically developed child *"Hey, you need to clean up that pigsty"* would usually be responded to with some humour. To a child with autism, this may simply totally confuse them – their bedroom is a bedroom, not a *"pigsty"*.

Step - By - Step: Always break down tasks into list type instructions. For example, instead of *"Come to the table now and sit down and* start eating your dinner so you finish in time to be able to get out to soccer practice" – an earful in anyone's terms, you need to break it down – "*Come to the table now*" – once at the table *"Now sit down in your chair"* – when sitting *"Eat all your dinner up"* – Now take your plate to the kitchen sink" – and so on. Naturally every child with autism is affected to differing degrees, so you need to customize the level of task breakdown according to your child's needs, but start simple and work your way up, rather than the other way around.

Visual Prompts: Use pictures of tasks needed to be performed on a regular basis.   That is, a picture of teeth being brushed in the bathroom, a picture of lying in bed sleeping in the bedroom, etc. You may also be using a picture exchange system for communication rather than just verbal prompts – if so, continue with this. You can also set up *visual lists of daily routines. For example, first picture is getting dressed, then one of having breakfast, then getting lunch/schoolbag, getting in taxi, etc. The person with autism can either remove the picture and place it on a blank card as they perform each task, or either they or you can put a whiteboard marker through each task as it is completed. Also note that real photos showing the actual items used, the environment they occur in, etc, are more effective than freehand drawn pictures. *(*Using laminated pictures with Velcro on the back of each, and a master card with the other side of the Velcro will allow you to change the pictures, and the person to remove the pictures as each task is completed).* NOTE: Some children and adults with autism do not need, nor respond well to the use of visuals, but I recommend they are at least tried – and if the child is not at all interested or responding to them in a positive way, then try alternative communication types (verbal, signs, gestures, etc).

Early Intervention and Social Skills Training: The earlier the age you start behavioural work with your child with autism, the more success is likely. Do not delay basic social skills training, as the quicker you make progress and the more often you prompt your child to use those skills the more likely the skills will be retained. On the next page are some basic guidelines around teaching new social skills to a child with autism.

- ✓ **Insist on eye contact:** A common feature of inappropriate social skills in a child with autism is their avoidance of eye contact. Don't fall into the *"That's just what people with autism do – so don't try and change it"* trap. That would be the same as accepting that husband's don't traditionally do the cooking, so don't try and change that, this is just nonsense. So your child does not become prompt reliant (that is, only makes eye contact when you say *"eyes"* or similar), use two different prompts. A verbal prompt of *"eyes"* or *"looking"*, paired with a physical prompt of placing your finger near their eyes and moving it towards your eyes is the best start. If the child refuses to make eye contact **gently** guide their face towards your direction until their eyes meet yours. Reinforce this immediately – *"Well done, great looking at eyes"*, and pair this initially with a tangible reinforcement like a piece of fruit or small piece of candy, or short play with a favourite toy. Do this every time you speak to your child or when your child is attempting to communicate with you. Slowly fade the verbal prompt to only every second time you use it, then every third time, etc until you need not say the prompt. Slowly change the physical prompt to a smaller and smaller physical motion until it is almost unnoticed by others, and then stop altogether. Remember to fade the prompts at the same speed of successful interactions, that is, ensure you are seeing some compliance before you start reducing the prompts. Be patient and consistent, do not give up after just a few days – it may take weeks or more with some children, but you will make progress if you remember to reinforce every success (also, fading the reinforcements when you are having some success of course).

- ✓ **Interrupting Self Stimulation Behaviour:** A common behaviour seen with people with autism, particularly children, is self-stimulation type behaviours (also termed stereotypical behaviours). These can include hand flapping, wiggling fingers in front of their eyes, spinning around either on their feet or sitting on the floor, regular hand clapping, lining up toys or other objects, hitting themselves regularly. Sometimes people again treat these behaviours as 'acceptable' because the person has autism, and so *"that's just what they do"*. Naturally these behaviours become stigmatising to the individual and also act as a barrier to learning new skills and taking part in purposeful and meaningful activities. The best action to take with these behaviours is actually quite simple; interrupt them as soon as they start. If they are lining up objects, move the objects around to break the line, also attempt to redirect to another more meaningful activity, continue doing this until they stop the lining up behaviour. Take the same approach with other self-stimming behaviours. If the behaviour is hand flapping, distract them with a favourite item or occupying their hands with objects that do not allow them to hand flap (incompatible behaviour).

- ✓ **Routine and Structure:** *Repeat this point ten times over.* The more routine and structure to the child's day and night, the higher the likelihood you will have less tantrums and behavioural incidents. Having set times for regular events like meals, bedtimes, and specific tasks like homework, etc, will be helpful in putting some order and control into their day and yours. However, on occasion vary these set times by around 15 minutes or so, to start teaching some tolerance around delays, and remember to reinforce 'good waiting' behaviour.

- ✓ **Teach 'How to Play':** Many children with autism, particularly children severely affected, will not know how to interact with toys or other children their age. You will need to teach play skills. Right from pushing a toy car back and forth and making *"vroom vroom"* noises, to building objects with toy blocks, you may need to teach each skill, step by step, reinforcing each correct response from your child. Teaching appropriate interactions such as *"Please play with me"* or

"Can I play with you" may also be necessary. If verbal language skills (talking) are not well developed, teaching appropriate physical gestures such as pointing, holding out their hand to receive an item, etc, will also be useful.

- ✓ **Generalise:** Wherever and whenever possible generalise the skills being taught. For example, if teaching road crossing skills don't just teach them on your road, use different roads at different times on different days. Also have them cross the road with more than just one person. When teaching play skills, as above, use different variations of toys. For example, if teaching how to play with a ball and it is red, you may find in future they will only play appropriately with balls that are red and not use any other colour ball. So, use different colours, sizes, and again ensure more than just one person teaches the skill and on different times of day.

- ✓ **Persistent and Consistent:** Don't let up on insisting the child follows the skills that have been taught. For example, if they have learnt appropriate greetings like *"Hello"* or *"Hi"*, or shaking hands when greeting someone, then ensure they do this every time as it will help that social skill become set and they will do this more naturally over time (though you may notice that social greetings, etc, may seem somewhat 'wooden' or unnatural in the way they sound, this is due to the person possibly never really fully understanding or accepting the necessity of these actions). *On a side note – do be aware that 'stranger danger' can be an issue with* children with autism. Because they often struggle to develop close relationships with people, that can also see them be too trusting or friendly towards strangers as understanding who to be close too and who not too is often a challenge.

Sensory Sensitivity

Some Parents and support people may be annoyed and concerned about why the child/adult they support who has autism insists of wearing certain clothes, or avoiding certain foods, etc. Often this is caused due to oversensitivity to a particular sensory sensation. For example, some people with autism may insist on only wearing clothes made out of fleece type material, this may be due to their skin being very sensitive to the roughness of other types of material. Some children/adults with autism may avoid any hard or crunchy foods, and only eat soft foods. This may be due to either the sound of eating hard foods being painfully loud to them or due to the texture of the food in their mouth being overbearingly uncomfortable. Auditory over-sensitivity is certainly a more common challenge for many with autism. Loud noises, many different noises occurring at the same time, high pitch or low pitch noises may all be very disturbing to someone with autism. They may tantrum, or run away trying to escape from what for some can actually be a painful experience. Keep this in mind when visiting shops or shows, try and visit when there are likely to be less people around, but don't avoid them altogether as building up tolerance to this stimuli is a necessity if the person is to learn to take part in activities in public areas as they get older.

Be aware of the sharks!

There are many people out there who try and 'make a buck' out of people with autism. All sorts of weird and wacky "cures", "treatments" and "therapies" are on offer, and unfortunately many of them are simply false hopes. Stick to scientifically proven (by reputable sources) approaches to autism. This author strongly recommends ABA based approaches, and certainly the Lovass based early intervention programmes. Even then, if you do find an ABA Therapist who offers to assist you with a behavioural programme, ask them what their qualifications are. Where did they get these qualifications from? Who have they worked with in the past, and what success was had? Early intervention programmes that claim they are Lovass based, yet only provide or recommend a few hours per week intervention are at worst nothing less than money making schemes, and at best well wishing semi-qualified 'Therapists' who don't realise they may be doing little to no good for the child and family.

Though any ABA intervention is better than nothing, studies clearly show that anything less than 40 hours per week (or close to it) very rarely results in any major improvements in learning new skills. Though you may see some early promising changes, the danger is the many weeks or months of a few hours here and there, is actually wasting valuable time where a full intensive programme could have been in place making definite and large improvement in the child's skill base.

Unwanted Behaviour, is Unwanted Behaviour

In this all too often politically correct World, a new approach or fad for want of a better term seems to be becoming common. That being "Let you child be autistic – they do what they do, because that's just how they are, and that's fine". I find myself becoming increasingly concerned and frustrated by this approach. No, you can't cure, as such, a child from Autism (though many snake oil sales people would argue otherwise), but you can teach appropriate behaviour and social skills to the vast majority of children with autism.

If a child with autism continually hits their head with their hand every time they are frustrated, then they are a child who is hitting their head – and that child happens to have autism. The new approach seems to be, "They are hitting their head because they have Autism". NO! Of course, their autism may lead them to becoming frustrated with people or other stimuli more easily, and their difficulty in communicating verbally may lead to them hitting their head to communicate how they are feeling, but it isn't the autism that makes them hit their head. Unwanted behaviour, is unwanted behaviour no matter who it is that is emitting that behaviour. In other words, don't full into the trap of excusing your child's behaviour because of their disability, or using their disability as an excuse not to do your job as a Parent and work on teaching wanted behaviour to replace the unwanted.

Fetal Alcohol Spectrum Disorder (FASD)

Fetal Alcohol Spectrum Disorder (FASD) is not a myth, and is not a small problem. Simply put, any alcohol a woman drinks during pregnancy *will pass into the placenta and subsequently through into the fetus.* Alcohol is a toxin, in other words it is actually poisonous to the human body and so does damage to bodies that can not efficiently process the alcohol out of their system quickly.

FASD is an all incorporating name that covers the different levels of effects that pre-natal exposure to alcohol can cause, those being: **Fetal Alcohol Syndrome** (FAS), **Fetal Alcohol Effects** (FAE), **Partial Fetal Alcohol Syndrome** (pFAS), **Alcohol Related Neurodevelopmental Disorders** (ARND), **Static Encephalopathy Alcohol Exposed** (SEAE) and **Alcohol Related Birth Defects** (ARBD). While some babies born with full FAS will have the characteristic physical features, which may include microcephalic head (small head, meaning smaller brain), small eye openings, small nose, smooth or lack of philtrum (line on upper lip), etc, others without the facial characteristics may still have the same brain damage and so face the same life long challenges.

There is no known safe amount of alcohol to drink while pregnant. Any amount at any stage of the pregnancy *may cause irreversible brain damage to the unborn baby.* Again, this is not a myth, yet the amount of ignorance and misinformation particularly in some smaller countries such as New Zealand leads people to believe that it is nothing to worry about and is just the latest 'pc' (politically correct) subject to push onto the public. Frighteningly there are even medical doctors who will tell pregnant women and others that it is perfectly safe to consume moderate amounts of alcohol while pregnant.

> *"There is no known safe amount of alcohol to drink while pregnant."*

A study by John Olney (Washington Medical School) showed that even two drinks during pregnancy may be enough to cause permanent brain damage, so **the myth that *"just one or two is fine"* is not correct at all**. (Addiction Biology 2004 Jun; 9(2):137-49).

The behavioural problems caused by FASD can be quite extensive and life affecting. Some of the more severe behavioural problems are as follows:

- ✓ **Difficulty connecting consequences to actions.** For example, one teenage girl with FASD (some years ago) was found to have taken a four year old cousin swimming late one night after climbing the swimming pool security fence. To start with they were having a good time, but soon the four year old became tired and began crying and wanting to go back home. The older girl, with FASD, quickly discovered that if she pushed the cousin's head under the water she didn't cry. This of course ended with the four year old drowning. The older girl appeared to never understand the connection between her pushing the toddlers head under the water and her subsequent death. To her she was simply stopping the crying, so how could her cousin's death be anything to do with her?

✓ **Lack of Impulse Control.** This means that often acting first and thinking later is a common issue. This is due to damage to a part of the brain called the Corpus Calossum, which joins the right half of the brain to the left half, allowing the two parts of the brain to communicate with each other. The left side of the brain processes facts, rules, logic, etc while the right side processes feelings, creativity and IMPULSES. So, if there is damage to the part of the brain that links these two hemispheres, often the right side of the brain acts independent of the left side and so facts and thought about possible consequences simply does not happen. So, act first, think later, is a reality sometimes for people with FASD.

✓ **Very concrete thinking, struggling with abstract terms.** The same girl as in the earlier example at one stage was being supported at a residential home for girls with challenging behaviour. However, she would regularly abscond from the house only to be picked up by the Police each time and returned. She continued the behaviour again and again, until one day someone asked her what it was about the rule she did not understand. After all, there were signs everywhere saying "No Running Away". The girl replied *"I'm not running away though. Each time I only walk, I don't run."* Keep in mind that the girl was not being sarcastic, she truly believed she wasn't breaking any rule, as how could her 'walking away' break the no 'running away' rule?

A person affected by FASD will also face many other challenges, including memory problems, understanding the concept of time (how long to wait, how long an activity lasts, when something occurred or will occur), and often forming inappropriate relationships with others. With all these challenges, it is no wonder that a very large percentage of people affected by FASD end up with interactions with law enforcement, and many also face mental health and addiction issues.

WHAT YOU CAN DO
BEHAVIOURAL PREVENTIONS and INTERVENTIONS for FASD

Patience, Tolerance and Repetition: It has been said that a child affected by FASD may need to hear the same description of how to perform a certain task up to a 1000 times before they retain the needed information. Some will cringe at this, but of course it does not mean repeating the same instruction a thousand times on the same day. But what it may mean for some children/adults affected is that just telling them two or three times about not touching the hot oven, will turn into telling them every single time the oven is on for years on end. Of course some will retain information quicker than others, so like any other disorder treat each person as an individual and adjust your instructions to the level they function at.

Avoid Slang and Euphemisms: Try to use language that is clear and free from slang. This author once worked with a young man affected by FASD and as part of a conversation I was having with him I had asked him to *"Just hang on a tick"* only to find him staring at me blankly and obviously confused. I quickly realised that he was trying to work out how on earth he could 'hang' on a 'tick', and why on earth would he need to?

Break Instructions into Small Steps: Too much information to process at once will result in much of it being forgotten before the FASD affected person has completed the task, meaning it is half completed or not done at all. Otherwise they may simply become very frustrated at not being able to understand what it is you are wanting them to do, and may emit behaviour that is challenging or even harmful to others. An instruction to *"Put your bag away in your bedroom and get your homework out, then go sit down and make a start then I'll bring you something to eat and drink"* will be too much to take in for many people affected by FASD. Instead, the instruction *"Put your bag in your bedroom now"* then when that is done *"Now take your homework out and take it on the table"*, and continuing in these small steps will be more successful.

Lists: What has also proved helpful is to list the tasks for the day, or better still for *parts* of the day. For example, have a morning list: 'Get dressed. Eat breakfast. Brush teeth. Lunch box in bag.' Then have another list for the afternoon and evening. The person can cross off each task as they perform it to help see what task they are up to next. For some people it may be better to use visual representations on these lists, such as a picture of clothes, breakfast, lunch box, etc. The list can be kept somewhere very visible to help them remember to use it, such as on the fridge door, or on their bedroom wall.

Routines and Structure: Routine makes tasks easier to remember and easier to follow. Try and have set times for daily activities such as 'get out of bed time' and sleep time, dinner time, etc. Where possible, do not vary from those times, not even for special events as any variance will often mean starting from scratch again the next day to re-establish the previously set routine. Variance in routine will also often cause upsets and frustration.

Environment: The Home, school, and even the workplace need to be as low in stimuli as possible. The more pictures, colours, movement, and sounds in the environment, the more distractions to prevent or slow the person's learning or task completion. Remember, FASD causes neurological damage and so the person affected will always struggle learning new information and keeping to task, so any distractions will simply make this even more difficult if not impossible. Remove posters, reduce noise when the person is on a specific task, and try and give them a space to work in where they are sheltered from the constant visual distractions of people moving back and forth.

FASD is a lifelong disorder, it doesn't go away .

These recommendations need to be taken account when the person is a child, adolescent and an adult. There is hope though, in that putting in place strong and consistent support networks (such as teachers, employers, friends and family) who know the issues the person faces, and what they can do to help them, the person can make some progress and live in a way that will keep them out of the justice system, and aid them in making friends and forming appropriate relationships.

NOTE: You will find some similarities between the behaviours and subsequent behavioural recommendations, to a person who has Autism or Aspergers Syndrome. It is true that that there are some similarities, but there are also some important differences. Where as around 50% of people with Autism can gain many skills if given appropriate and effective early intervention, people affected by FASD will have much slower success and less advancements in their skills because of their sometimes severe brain damage. There are also a large percentage of wrong diagnoses handed out by pediatricians and others who mistake FASD for autism, ADHD, Aspergers or other condition.

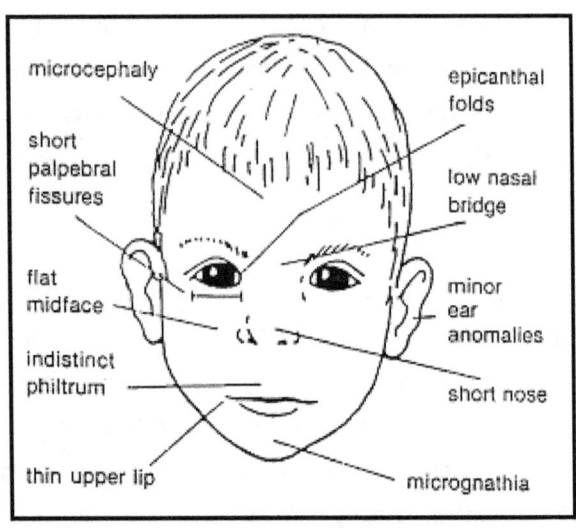

"While some babies born with full FAS will have the characteristic physical features, which may include microcephalic head (small head, meaning smaller brain), small eye openings, small nose, smooth or lack of philtrum (line on upper lip), etc, others without the facial characteristics may still have the same brain damage and so face the same life long challenges."

The Dior Method
ANALYSE AND MODIFY YOUR CHILD'S BEHAVIOUR

The data from the ABCR discussed earlier is in fact very important, and behaviour analysts will use this as part of their assessment process to recommend strategies in modification of the behaviours of concern. However, the *'Dior Method'* incorporates one extra set of data, that helps with Parents, and support people working out what it is that is going on with the person they are supporting. We refer to the set of data to be analysed as the **ABCR**.

Before we explain what the **ABCR** stands for, and why you must understand these to some degree, you need to be prepared for collecting some basic data that will help you understand (we hope) what it may be that is maintaining your child's unwanted behaviour. Further in this chapter is a data collection sheet that you should use to collect some basic *baseline data (*data collected before any specific strategy is implemented), and later, some post-strategy data. This will give you information to work on and think about in regards to how you approach this issue by way of following the *Dior Method*, and a way to really measure the success of the strategies implemented.

ABCR

- **A** – Refers to the **antecedents** of the behaviour displayed. That is, what happened immediately before the behaviour occurred? If there appeared to be nothing unusual, what happened within 30 minutes of the behaviour (or further back if needed)? Was the child verbally teased, did they injure themselves, were they refused a request? What was it that occurred in this time? It may seem insignificant at first to note these things down, but it may be an important part of the solution later.

- **B** – Refers to the **behaviour** you observed. Not what you think they did, or think they said, but *what you actually saw, and heard* (and maybe felt). Describe and think about exactly what it was you observed.

- **C** – Refers to the **consequence**. Our definition of consequence differs a little when using the *Dior Method* – compared to the standard ABC definition. You want to know what the consequence was to the child for displaying that specific behaviour. This is difficult and be warned you can easily show your bias if you are not completely subjective here. You must note down what it was that you saw at the end of the behavioural incident (B.I.). What did they get out of the behaviour? In other words, what observable things happened? E.g. People looking at them, people shouting at them, being picked up, etc.

- **R** – Response from you. That is, what did you do during and immediately after the B.I.? For example, was the child verbally reprimanded, given a sweet, toy, game? Was the child put into time out, if so what room did they get put into and for how long.

The **R,** or response (reinforcement), is the most important of all factors in this data, and the most important part of what will determine the likelihood of that behaviour being repeated. That is, receiving something you like, or value immediately after a specific behaviour will increase the likelihood you will repeat it. For example, receiving the comments *"Great Job, that's a bonus for you this week"* from your Boss, will increase the likelihood you will put in extra effort next time. If your boss says nothing, or says *"About time you finished that",* it is unlikely you will put in as much effort next time.

To make the rest of this behaviour modification information a little more user friendly, we will use a fictional child as a model. This child's name is Freddy. Freddy is six years old, of average intellectual ability and in good health.

To look at how our actions, immediately after a behavioural incident (B.I.), affect the likelihood of that behaviour being repeated in the future, lets look at Freddy's first visit to a supermarket.

> On the way around the supermarket Dad goes down the confectionery aisle. Freddy sees the chocolate bars and asks Dad if he can have one. Dad tells him "No, it's not good for you Freddy; you can have some muesli bars though". With this, Freddy responds by screaming, stamping his fists on the trolley, and falling to the floor refusing to get up when Dad tries to move him along. Faced with the embarrassment of everyone staring at him, Dad gives Freddy the chocolate bar, and Freddy stops his B.I.

Now let's looks at the ABCR data we would have recorded if we had been observing:

A (antecedent) – Seeing chocolate bars, and Dad saying *"no"* to chocolate bar request

B (behaviour) – Screaming for 2 minutes, banging fists 10 – 12 times on trolley, rolling on the floor

C (consequence) – Dad pleads with him to stop, people walking past stare, Dad looks uncomfortable.

R – Dad gave Freddy chocolate bar
Freddy has just learnt that screaming, banging fists and rolling on the floor results in receiving a chocolate bar if in the supermarket with Dad. Freddy may also generalize this event into other parts of his life – that is, next time he wants something he may very well display the same behaviour if he does not get what he wants.

Using the first stage of the *Dior Method* (data analysis), on the following page, we list the key observable events from each of the four categories, A,B,C, and R.

"... receiving something you like, or value immediately after a specific behaviour, will increase the likelihood you will repeat it"

DATA ANALYSIS

Stage One of the '*Dior Method'*

Taking our data from Freddy's visit to the supermarket we do the following:

1) - Note actual observable antecedent (A), if known.

> **A** = seeing chocolate bars, and being told *"no"* (this comes under **compliance**)

2) – Note behaviours observed

> **B** = screaming, shouting, banging fists, rolling on floor (this comes under **tantrums**)

3) – Note consequence to child

> **C** = Dad talking to him and people looking at him (this comes under the **attention** category)

4) – Now we look at the response

> **R** = given chocolate bar (**tangible reward**)

The importance of collecting the data is to enable you to work out which of the *Dior Method* analysis categories each of the stages of a B.I. belong to, and thus enabling you to refer to the recommended behaviour modification strategies that are described later in the chapter.

It is essential also that you remember **all behaviours have a function to the person emitting the behaviour.** Subsequently we need to try and figure out what exactly that function is, and replace the unwanted behaviour with a more acceptable behaviour. With some unwanted behaviour it is fairly straight forward to discover what the function is. With the supermarket visit described previously, the function of Freddy's behaviour was to obtain a chocolate bar. Our challenge now is to find a way to change his screaming, shouting and fist banging to requesting a chocolate bar verbally, and accepting "no" as the answer without resorting to the unwanted behaviours again.

We can see above that the function of Freddy's behaviour was to obtain attention (from anyone who would listen!), and the response was Dad giving him a chocolate bar. So, we need to give Freddy other ways to get attention that are acceptable. Teaching him, at home, to say *"Dad can I please have a chocolate bar"*, and rewarding him by saying *"That's a great way to ask Freddy, well done. This time we can't have a bar, but maybe next time we visit you can".* You will need to role-play this several times. Along with this, you will need some patience and tolerance of Freddy and others. The next time Freddy screams for a bar in the supermarket, you will need to ignore this behaviour. Do not give in, do not react whatsoever, continue as per normal. To start with Freddy may yell louder and more frequent, but in time the behaviour will reduce or stop.

All behaviour has a function to the person performing it. By using the Dior Method of data analysis, you may be able to work out what the function is, and which strategy to trial. Often ignoring unwanted behaviour is a part of the solution. Patience is needed

Use the following tables to record your child's unwanted behaviour/s. If more than one behaviour, use another set of tables. Use the example's explained above as a guide to what you are looking for to record down. The first graph will act as our baseline (giving you data to compare with after the strategy has been in place for at least four weeks, to see if progress has been made). Preferably you will wait until you have four sets of data in the baseline, then compare that data for similarities and use the most common factors in the data analysis page (which follows). The second and third graph can be used for recording data during the strategy's use, and the fourth for after four weeks of running the strategy.

Baseline Data
(before you try any strategies)

Date / Time	Antecedent/s	Behaviour	Consequence	Response

First Week of Strategy

Date / Time	Antecedent/s	Behaviour	Consequence	Response

Second Week of Strategy

Date / Time	Antecedent/s	Behaviour	Consequence	Response

Fourth Week of Strategy

Date / Time	Antecedent/s	Behaviour	Consequence	Response

IMPORTANT NOTES: When recording baseline data, try not to have anything done differently from the way the situation is usually handled. This way you can get a more accurate comparison between pre-strategy behaviour levels, and post-strategy behaviour levels.

Remember to only record what you actually observe (what you SEE, Hear, SMELL, FEEL) not what you assume happened, or making judgments about why it happened.

Behaviour Categories

You can now categorise your data using the following ABCR descriptors. Again, this will help you decide on which behaviour modification strategy to use, and to find further information in the **glossary of terms.**

A	Being refused request, item taken away after warnings given	*Compliance*
A	Asked to perform specific task, performing task then suddenly stopping.	*Task demand*
A	Specific person/people arrive, specific sound/smell/tactile activity	*Sensory Sensitivity*
A	Other	*Other*

B	Screaming or shouting "No", "Don't want to", "I won't", or displaying other refusal type verbal behaviour (i.e. speaking) or by physical gesture (e.g. shaking head)	*Non - Compliance*
B	Banging head, scratching self, slapping or punching self. Other behaviours aimed at causing pain/injury to themself.	*Self Injurious Behaviour*
B	Hitting out at others, throwing items, breaking items purposely	*Tantrums*
B	Other	*Other*

C	Gaining attention of others (either by them looking at them, listening to them, touching them)	*Attention*
C	Task demanded of them not having to be done	*Escaping Task Demand*
C	Person or people in their environment move away from them or leave (at time of B.I.)	*Escape Specific Attention*

The **R** category we do not separate into categories as we have done with the previous three categories. Instead, we cover the **response** separately

Your Response (Reinforcement)

The R category is by far the most important factor that you need to focus on if you wish to modify your child's behaviour.

What you do during and <u>immediately after</u> a behavioural incident will determine the likelihood of that behaviour being repeated in the future. Keeping this in mind, we can change how we respond to firstly decrease the likelihood of an unwanted behaviour reoccurring and secondly to increase the likelihood of a wanted behaviour occurring.

This sounds easy enough, but actually working out what the response is that may be inadvertently reinforcing your child's unwanted behaviour, and then changing this to a response that does not do this can actually be quite difficult.

Let's now start using those data categories shown above, to work out which strategy to use.

By now you should have collected the data in your baseline chart (if not, do not continue with these steps until you have).

If your data shows: **Compliance,** and/or **Task command,** as the antecedents (**A**), and/or your child displays behaviour that falls into the **Non-Compliance** data category of the behaviour (**B**) table, and/or the **escaping task demand** in the consequences (**C**) category, then you first need to ascertain whether the task being asked of the child is actually understood by them.

Strategy One – Compliance Issues

Approach your child when they are calm. Settle them and make them comfortable, sometimes a short low stimulus game or activity (like drawing) can achieve this. Now ask them to explain to you what it was you asked them to do earlier (before the B.I. occurred). If they can't explain it clearly (or demonstrate parts of it if non-verbal), or they really do not seem to know what you are asking, you need to look at breaking the task request into smaller and simpler steps.

If you say to your child *"Ok, now please go and clean up your room before you do your homework, then you can watch TV",* and this results in a B.I., you need to break it down. I.e." *Hey, how about going to your room now. Pick up ten things from the floor, and let me know when you have done that".* When this is achieved, reinforce the good behaviour. *"Great, what a good job you did. (Wait a moment, then -) Ok, now see if you can get all the red Lego bricks in the bucket, let me know when you have done this – you are so fast!".*

You can see that we have made a once seemingly nightmarish task become lots of fun little challenges. You have also shown your child you are proud of the little things they accomplish, and also enabled them to see sometimes doing jobs can be fun.

Does your child understand the tasks you ask them to do? Get them to explain the task to you (or demonstrate parts of it if non-verbal). Break the task into small fun steps.

If your child knows what you asked of them, and they simply do not want to do it, then again you first follow the recommended strategy (Strategy One – Compliance Issues). Attempt to turn the once horrible task, into small fun tasks. If this is not successful, then we need to show our authority, and that refusal to perform a reasonable, fair, achievable and understood task will not be accepted.

We are NOT, however, going to use any form of punishment, as the *Dior Method* is completely non-aversive (non-punishment based), we do however sometimes utilize what is termed 'response cost' which will be explained a little further on. To show our 'authority', we use Strategy Two – Compliance Issues. This comprises of doing the following when a reasonable task request results in a B.I. Like all the strategies outlined in this chapter, consistency of approach is of utmost importance. You must follow these steps each time, and exactly as outlined, as must anyone else who may deal with unwanted behaviour shown by your child for these antecedents.

Strategy Two – Compliance Issues

1) Explain the task clearly, calmly but firmly (**never** shout, swear or threaten). Always ensure your task requests are 'clear but fair'. If the Child begins to display unwanted behaviour –

2) Explain the task again, firmly but calmly. Now walk away for 2-3 minutes, where the child can not see or hear you.

3) Now return. If the child has still not performed the task, ask the child *"Why have you not done what I have asked you, did you understand what it was I asked?"* Give them a chance to respond, and listen to what they have to say. However, do not answer questions that are not related to the task itself. Do not enter into bargaining (e.g. *"I will pick up my clothes, if you give me my pocket money"*). Also, do not enter into a power struggle (i.e. do not start arguing about whether they should or should not have to do this task). Instead, provide, calmly, any clarification of the task that is needed. If the task was understood, simply say *"I have heard what you have said, now please do the job which is to ………."*. Now walk away for 5 minutes (if possible or at least 1 minute if you are under time pressures). Return again, if the task has not been started then –

4) Say *"You have not done what I have asked"*. Now escort the child calmly but firmly to a no-low stimulus area. This may be the bathroom or laundry (somewhere where they do not have access to toys, etc – **but do not put them in rooms where there is**

poisonous material readily available if they are under five years old, or have an intellectual or developmental disability!). Have them stand there, or sit, for 1 minute for every year of age (up to a maximum of ten minutes). During this time do not interact with them at all (say nothing; do not look directly at them). You can use your body to block their exit from this area, as long as it will not cause injury to them or yourself. **Do NOT ever lock a child in a room. Do NOT leave the child unattended in this area.** When the time is up, calmly but firmly escort them back to the area they were in, and repeat the task as originally asked. Do not enter into any further discussions. Follow the steps from 1 through to four again if necessary until the task is completed. Do not give in, or once again, your child learns they can 'win'.

Always speak in a calm but firm voice. Do not enter into arguments or bargaining; be 'fair and clear'. Always stay calm, do not lose your temper – your child learns from you.

<u>*If your data shows:*</u> **Sensory Sensitivity** as the antecedent, you will need to try the following strategy: Strategy Three – Sensory Sensitivity.

Strategy Three – Sensory Sensitivity

You need to help lower your child's anxiety-related behaviours about being round certain people, in certain environments, or specific noises, etc, by pairing them with positive reinforcers. That is, associating something good, with the situation (person, object, stimuli) once feared or disliked.

1) You need to start very small. Firstly, just talk about the feared stimuli. For example if it was the fear of cats that triggered the unwanted behaviour - *"How big is a cat when it is first born? How big does it get when it is an adult? Are cats soft or hard?"* For every reply the child gives you about his/her feared stimuli, reward them with verbal praise *"Well done! That's right!"* Pair this with another reinforcer, like a small sweet or short play with a special toy, etc.

2) You may want to repeat step one – three or four times, slowly talking a little more about the stimuli. Now carry on with the process in step one, but also start talking about imagining being in the same environment with that stimuli. You may also need to help your child relax as they start trying to imagine this. For example, have them lie down, you can hold their hand and/or stroke their hair as they imagine the scene you describe. Also once again start small, for example: *"Imagine you are in a room with a big glass wall in the middle. On the other side of the glass wall, is a beautiful*

soft fluffy white cat." You would then in subsequent sessions describe closer contact, with half a glass wall – bending over the wall to pat the top of the cat, and so on. If your child gets upset at this at any time - stop and reassure them everything is ok, *"we are only imagining"*. You may then need to revert back to step one for some time.

3) Introduce pictures of the stimuli – in this example, a picture of a cat (start with a small kitten, then work your way up). Then take them to environments where they can see the stimuli in real life, maybe at a distance first. Eventually, over further sessions, bring them closer and closer to the feared stimuli.

Obviously **if it is a specific person or people the child dislikes,** you will need to alter this process a little. Do this by first discussing what things your child likes about that person (even if it is just their hair!). Then what it is they dislike. Use the reinforcers for positive things your child can think of about the person. Have the person speak to them on the phone to start with – even just a hello, then go from there. *As a side note – always consider there may be a hidden reason your child is not telling you about for why they fear/dislike that person (first thing you can do is ask what they do not like about that person – only after you have gone through what they do like) consider the possibility of abuse issues, or otherwise – but do not ask leading questions or become paranoid. If you have any real concerns like this,* **always consult a professional.**

If your child is displaying **self-injurious behaviour**, this is obviously a serious issue. Though some behaviours like head banging, pinching self, and sometimes hair pulling are not that uncommon in younger children (2 – 4 year olds), if the behaviour occurs frequently or at a high rate (more than three times in a fortnight, or has continued infrequently longer than three months) you **should seek professional assistance immediately.** At the very least, discuss your concerns with your GP, and tell them the full extent of the behaviour, do not be ashamed of telling them exactly what your child is doing. If the behaviour is infrequent, and not causing any injury to the child, **ignore the behaviour.** Each time the child engages in the self-injurious type behaviour, turn away from them; do not speak to them until, at least one minute after they stop. **Do this every time.**

Note: See the warning about this procedure (often called extinction) in the chapter about extinction.

The Dior Method
TOILET TRAINING

*Image by **Emma Lewis***

Need to Know Terms:

Void – **to rid oneself of waste either by urination or by bowel motion.**

Positive reinforcer – **a reinforcer is something special that the child enjoys having access to (special toy, book, music, drink). Naturally one for the toilet should be something that can be kept there hygienically.**

Positively reinforce – **reward the individual in a way that they will feel good. This may be saying well done, it may be access to a special toy, or a special snack**

Secondary Reinforcer – **a reinforcer (treat) that is in addition to verbal praise**

Cue – **A hint, sign or indication**

Generalise – **to take the behaviour into other environments, other times, for other people**

Hand-over-hand prompting – **placing your hand lightly on the hand or arm of the person being trained, and gently guiding their motions to achieve the task being taught.**

Fading – **slowly reducing the amount of reinforcers supplied or prompts given**

Note: *The strategies described in this chapter are for both males and females. We sometimes use the term 'her, she' or 'him, he' but these are not an indication that the strategy is for only a female or only a male, more so to help with grammatical flow.*

Toilet training could be one of the most stressful events parents and children go through in the early years. Yet it need not be a drawn out issue, and in many cases – even with developmentally delayed children, can be resolved within a week, and sometimes less.

The three strategies outlined in this book can be used with typically developed children or with children with an intellectual or developmental disability. Also included are short chapters specifically addressing issues faced by Parents who have a child with autism, or with an intellectual disability. Parents of neuro-typical children may also find some of the information in those chapters is also helpful when addressing specific issues their child may be having with toilet training.

Important Issues

Before you decide to embark on a toilet training mission with your child, you need to give some thought to the following:

- **Is your child at both a chronological and developmental age where you can reasonably expect her to accept and be able to learn all the facets that toileting consists of?**

Interestingly when researching the average age that a typically developed child is ready for toilet training, we found a wide range of ages quoted. Anywhere from 18 months to 32 months were recorded as so-called 'average ages'. However, by far, and in agreement with our own knowledge, around 24 months of age for girls, and slightly older for boys (28 months) would be the average chronological age. Keep in mind if your child is developmentally delayed, she may need to be older before she is ready for this training. Also remember that every child is different! There is not necessarily a right or wrong age to toilet train. Different cultures also vary with toilet training ages. Many children with autism may not be fully toilet trained up until they are 4 or even 5 years of age due to developmental considerations and challenges. However, we recommend that at a maximum age to at least attempt a toilet training programme with - for any child disabled or not, is three and a half years of age.

- **Is your child having longer periods of dry nappies?**

If they are now waiting up to 3 hours or so before wetting, that would indicate they have at least some bladder control, and it is likely they can differentiate between a dry nappy (pants) and wet.

- ❏ ***Disposables verses cloth nappies.**

*A little to late now to make any changes, however keep in mind that disposable nappies are now very effective in keeping moisture away from babies skin. So, if your child has been wearing only disposables in the months preceding your embarking on toilet training her, you may have a slightly tougher time.

Cloth nappies, obviously by the nature of the material, are immediately dampened when a child urinates, and so the child can sense the change from dry to wet, thus aiding their understanding about voiding (toileting). However, do not be dismayed if you have been a firm user of disposables for your children (as the authors have been with most of theirs) all is not lost!

- ❏ **Potty or toilet?**

Please, please, please ...... forget using potties! The number of training books and leaflets so called 'childhealth experts' write, who start off any toilet training advice talking about using a potty, is surprising and a little frightening. We strongly recommend that unless there is a specific physiological reason, or your child is disturbingly terrified of sitting on the toilet, you do not use potties and DO use the toilet itself as the first and only toileting equipment. It makes no sense to spend much time and effort training your child to use a potty, to then only spend more time moving her from potty to toilet bowl. For those still not convinced, think it through logically. Remember when you first learnt to drive, did you spend hours upon hours sitting on a kitchen chair with a toy steering wheel and a wooden spoon gearstick, 'learning' how to drive, or did you start first off in a driving instructor's vehicle (or a brave family member's car!)? However, there are toilet seat inserts, that make the seat area smaller (so the child feels more comfortable and secure – and doesn't fall down the hole!).

- **Compliance. Is your child currently compliant with most reasonable requests made of it?**

If your child will come to you when you call, and follow a basic request like "pick up the spoon" or "put kitten down" on at least 50% of occasions, you can accept your child is at least averagely compliant. This will certainly help the toileting process, as requests to stay on the toilet or to wipe their bottom will be made by you and you will have your, and their stress levels greatly reduced if you have reasonable compliance. If you currently have little to no compliance from your child, these strategies will be difficult to implement. If you feel that your child complies with little to no requests you make of it, more common with children with moderate or worse autism and other developmental delays (though not unique to), we suggest you refer back to the chapter on obtaining compliance (Chapter #) before you begin on using any of the toileting strategies. However, do not rule out toilet training at this time if you feel your child is far from compliant, you may still have success using the strategies supplied as they are designed with the most challenging child in mind.

❑ **Which of the three strategies should you use?**

This is really only a question you can answer. The strategies all follow the same basic principles of scheduling (whether it be fixed or to responses observed), and reinforcement. Yet one child may respond quickly to one strategy and not at all to others, where another child may respond to the others but not to that one. We suggest you read through each of them, discuss with your partner or fellow support person, and decide on which one is more likely to succeed taking into account your day-to-day demands of life, and your child's challenges. Though there is no reason you can not try one, and then another if you appear to be having no success, we do recommend you give some thought to the one you try first, because if it backfires and turns to disaster this may influence your child's future thinking about using the toilet and make other attempts at training more difficult. Also, strategy three ('Sit and wait') is more aimed at children who may be having some trouble with identifying the bladder full sensation or the sensation before a bowel movement. If you really can not decide, and feel this really is going to be a mission, we suggest you trial strategy One (using the 'Dior Method'), as this uses some extra principles to the other two, that in most cases will see quick success – though a little more energy draining for the parent or support person!

- **Equipment?**

Other than a standard toilet, and maybe a fit-in-toilet seat for toddlers, you need nothing else but lots of patience and a calm demeanour. Remember, we advise against potties.

The 'Dior Method'

This 'Dior Method' relies on your powers of observation, and more importantly on how well you know your child's behaviours, and behavioural cues. That is, being able to recognise what your child usually does just before they void. This may be a certain facial expression, total silence and/or stillness, taking themselves to a corner of the room, holding their groin area, a certain movement or posture, etc. If you do not already have an idea of what your child does just before voiding, you will need to carefully observe them over the period of a day or two, taking mental (or written) note of what they did just before they wet or soiled their nappy.

This strategy is one that needs to be run over two or more consecutive days until you have reached success. It is not recommended for just an hour or two now, and another hour later – maybe tomorrow. So plan what two days (maybe more) you will have your child at home with little to no distraction. Preferably days where you do not need to rush off at some stage, and have to put nappies back on the child before you have reached the stage where you want to be that day. In saying that, you can plan for an outing that day as long as you have finished the work for that day (nappy off time) with a success, voiding in the toilet.

Step One

This strategy uses what we term The 'Dior Method'. What this means is, it has had specific strategies added to it that will help the process being learnt. The 'Dior Method' uses scientifically based principles of positive reinforcement, combined with repetition, environmental enhancement and behaviour analysis. Don't let these terms baffle you or concern you, these principles are simply added into the strategy that you are about to read through – and then implement.

You will need to have your child free of their nappies for the day. Obviously if it is summertime, or you can have the house warm by means other than the sun, this is best. We want to make the house environment as comfortable as possible. This includes the toilet. Nothing will put your child off more than a freezing cold loo in a nice warm house! What we also now recommend you do is add some 'extras' to the toilet room itself. That is, make it attractive to your child. Put one or two posters on the wall that your child loves to look at, maybe a favourite book placed on a string attached to the wall, so it can only be looked at while in the toilet. Ensure the toilet smells nice, even us adults don't like going into a smelly loo! An air freshener will do nicely here, or for a short lasting more child friendly smell, a dab or two of vanilla essence on a small piece of cloth sitting on the windowsill or elsewhere in the toilet will help make the room nicer to visit. Do not fear though – you do not need to keep these 'added extras' there permanently, just for the period of training and for around three to four weeks after the training has been successful.

You now also need to decide on at least two different special reinforcers. These may be special toys that he can play with for three or four minutes after a success, or it may be a special edible treat like three or four M+M's, or similar. The most important thing here is, your child will greatly enjoy this special treat as it is something they usually rarely get. You must also remember that when you do provide this special reinforcer after a success, it must be limited – so they do not get so used to having it they are not interested next time, which is why we say three or four M+M's rather than a pack!

Other than having the child's nappy removed, do not drastically change the rest of the normal daily routine, other than you suddenly taking an even bigger interest in watching them play than usual.

Step Two

Monitor your child every minute. As soon as it appears they are about to void, pick them up gently but quickly and walk with them straight to the toilet. While holding them, and in those few seconds it takes for you to reach them and pick them up, say "Wait, wait, wait*......" and continue this until after having placed them on the toilet itself. If any of the urine or bowel motion actually does go into the bowl (which is the main goal of course) make a really big deal about it. "Great, fantastic, what a good girl, well done"! Lots of hugs and smiles, and have that special reinforcer <u>available right then and</u>

there. It is <u>very</u> important you provide that special reinforcer almost immediately, so they connect the positive behaviour (voiding in the toilet) with a positive even afterwards (access to that special toy, the special snack, etc). *Though your child may not understand what 'wait' means at this time, in most cases they will soon connect the word 'wait' with the message you are trying to get across..

If by the time you reach the toilet, they have already voided (yes, unfortunately this may happen – and most likely more than once), still sit them on the toilet for at least two minutes. It is important your child relates voiding with sitting on the toilet. This will also help them get used to sitting on the toilet. Do not tell them off if they have already voided before reaching the toilet. You can however say, "Nearly made it, next time you will make it". Be calm, though this is hard when you may have a mess to clean up, it is important as your child will pick up on any negative comments, facial expressions, or movements you make and this may make them think of the toilet as a scary negative place. Unfortunately you do not let them have the special reinforcer if they did not void into the toilet, but do not make a big deal about this (i.e. do NOT say "you can't have your treat now", as this will just start to create stress around the whole issue of toileting, and create more of a challenge).

Step Three
Eventually you should see your child start moving towards the toilet themselves when they need to void, and you need only take their

hand and calmly but quickly walk with them (not pull them) to the toilet, and assist them when there - if needed.

Step Four

Once your child has voided successfully three times in succession (all in the toilet bowl), they can now 'graduate' to wearing undies. Keep in mind though, even though they are now in undies rather than nappies, you may need to keep repeating step one, two and three until you have more dry times than wet. Remember to get them to pull their pants down by themselves once in the toilet, though you may need to help them a little the first one or two times. Also cue them to wipe their bottom, pull pants up, and flush the toilet by themself (where physically possible of course). Again remember the 'well done, fantastic,' comments and the special reinforcer access. However, it is also now time to start fading the reinforcers. Start with the special reinforcer, only presenting it for access maybe every second occasion, then every third, then either at random, or stop completely. If your child is not able to do these tasks (pulling pants down, wiping, pants up, etc), provide some hand-over-hand prompting and fade as time progresses (See Chapter # for a full explanation of hand-over-hand prompting and how to fade prompts).

Step Five

Remember to generalise. Once your child has achieved success in reaching the 'underwear on' stage, start exposing them to other environments (fully clothed obviously!). For example - shopping malls, libraries, houses of friends and family. When arriving, show your child where the toilet is there. The first two or three visits to each location you may need to monitor them fairly closely to watch for behaviour that suggests they may need to void soon, if so, prompt them to go to the toilet. Even at a friend's house, support them by going with them the two or three times, remember new toilet – added stress. Particularly children with autism or aspergers may find using another toilet very stressful, as it is different from the routine and environment they were used to (See chapter # on autism). Again remember to give lots of positive verbal reinforcement in the new environment, so they know you are pleased when they use other toilets as well as the one at home. Try and share the training between support people as well. For example: your partner, other caregivers, grandparents, older siblings, etc. It is important that your child toilets for others and not just you!

WHAT IF ...

"I just can't work out the cues, she just seems to go wee whenever and wherever"

Then you need to see if your partner, or other caregivers have noticed any specific little behaviour that she does before voiding. It may even be as simple as making eye contact, or avoiding eye contact. If you really can't find those cues though, you would be better off trying one of the other two strategies.

"He gets really upset when I pick him up and take him to the toilet"

Unfortunately you just need to work through this one. Same old story, ignore the unwanted behaviour – positively reinforce the wanted behaviour. However, ensure you are not frightening your child by the way you are picking them up and rushing them there. Though you do need to act quickly, to avoid a mess and increase chances of success, if it becomes a very frightening experience this could well achieve the opposite of what you want. That is, your child becomes terrified of the bladder/bowel–full feeling, and of going to the toilet! You could try making it a fun experience, singing a favourite song or nursery rhyme on the way to the toilet is one method, rather than using the 'wait, wait' prompt. Remember though, as you get some success you will need to fade this singing or game-play.

Strategy Two – Sit and Wait

This strategy can see toilet training completed within one to two days, even with many children who have a moderate to severe developmental delay. Yet it takes much patience by both you and your child! It may also be somewhat stressful for you both, though shared between two to three people – will not take to much of a toll on you, and if the child is supplied with enough toys, books, etc (as detailed below) should not be too stressful for them either.

Step One

Set up a seat in, or at the door, of the toilet. This seat is for you, or the caregiver talking their turn supporting your child. Also place in or just at the door a box of favourite toys, books, puzzles, etc (no not yours, your child's!). Also have handy (though not in the toilet area yet) a seat for your child, for him to sit on a little further along in the process.

Step Two

Immediately after having breakfast, <u>including a drink</u>, sit your child on the toilet, with you sitting on your seat near them. Obviously, do not have him wearing nappies or pants during this process. Give him a toy or book to play with, and encourage him to stay on the toilet seat. As soon as he voids, provide those great verbal reinforcements immediately "Great, fantastic, what a good boy, well done, you did wee/poo in the toilet that's so good"! Help him wipe himself if needed, and now put undies on him (yes, straight into undies with this strategy, no nappies at the moment! You can now also give him a fifteen-minute reprieve from sitting on the toilet. Let him go and do whatever he wishes too. However, in the last five minutes, prompt him again to have a drink (preferably at least half a glass). Provide whatever needed to ensure he will drink it, yes even the dreaded soft drink - just for this exercise. After the fifteen-minute break – you guessed it, back to sitting on the toilet. They need to sit there until they void again, then repeat the process again, fifteen-minute break, drink, etc.

Step Three

Once the child has voided at least four times, on the fifth session, place them on a chair next to the toilet seat. Watch for cues that they may be about to void, or if they start voiding on the chair itself, quickly but calmly lift them onto the toilet bowl (hopefully, he will get up off the seat and get onto the toilet unprompted and void in there!). If over 50% of the void goes into the bowl, again provide the positive reinforcers and the fifteen-minute break. If most goes on the seat or floor, clean them up – say nothing, and sit them back down on their seat, do not appear or act angry or upset, but at the same time do not make eye contact or say anything for at least a minute or two (though if they are overly upset, it is ok to calm them as you need to, but make this as short as possible). You may now need to provide another drink to initiate more urination. If you have more than three 'misses' in a row, go back to step one – sitting them on the actual toilet until they void in there. Wait again until you get two voids in the bowl, then back to sitting on the seat, repeating this step again.

Step Four

When you have achieved two successes, with your child getting up off the seat to void in the toilet bowl, now move his seat about four feet (just over a metre) away from the toilet bowl, and continue the sessions – breaks after successful voids can now be twenty minutes long. Each time you have a success, move the seat (and yours) another four feet away from the toilet. You should now also be prompting him to wipe himself, and pull pants up by himself (use hand-over-hand prompting if needed). When you (and your child) are really achieving great things – with his chair around twenty feet from the toilet, increase the breaks from twenty to around thirty minutes, again with a drink in those last few minutes.

Step Five

Once you are over the twenty feet mark, simply loose the chair altogether, and simply provide a verbal prompt about every thirty minutes for "toilet time", you may need to take his hand and lead him here for the first one or two times, just to get him used to walking there from any part of the house, rather than just from the chair he was on. Continue with the verbal reinforcement, but slowly fading it now.

"Each time you have a success, move the seat (and yours) another four feet away from the toilet"

You should now nearly have a toilet-trained child! However, yes things may not run as smooth as we would want, and you may have to run the sessions over a period of two days or more until you get to the desired level of consistency of voiding in the toilet. If you are not having any success with your child self-initiating sitting on the toilet to void, from the seat you have placed them on, after say five attempts on the chair, and you have gone back to step one before trying the second step again, have a break for say two hours, then return again to step one and start over. Yes, you do need lots of patience!

If your child is becoming extremely anxious over sitting on the toilet bowl right from the first session of an extended period of time, despite your attempts to amuse her with toys and books from the box you have, you may need to try a desensitisation process with the toilet to start with (see desensitising notes at end of this chapter). Once the desensitising process is finished, then come back to this strategy.

WHAT IF ...

'After ten minutes he is sick of sitting on the toilet, and tantrums to such a degree I can not get him to stay there'

This is tough, though we really need them to stay on until success (and you should work through this if you can), we also <u>do not want the experience of being on the toilet to be a negative one!</u> If your best attempts to engage them in what you have there for them fails, let them go to where they want to go! However, do not let them have access to other items they want that are not in the toilet (i.e. watching TV, playing on the playground, etc). If the things outside of the toilet are so much more fun, and they can access them just by tantruming, they will do it again and again. While they are settling down, reassess what items you have there in the toilet area that will be of interest, are they really his favourite things? Is there a game you can play while he sits there, nursery rhymes to sing, photo albums to look through, etc? Once you have found some more interesting and 'exciting' activities, and he has calmed right down, try again.

If still tantruming to such a degree you have to let him go again, this time – once he is calm, 'prime him' with lots and lots of drinks! Once he can't get another drop down*, take him to the toilet again, and this time insist he stays there, nature will quickly take its course and he will urinate in the bowl while there, even if tantruming at the time. But that's ok – you have had a success! Provide the verbal reinforcement, special reinforcers, and let him have his break. He now knows, weeing in the loo equals nice things! Next time, the tantrums should be less, if not, again repeat what we have just suggested.

> **Please be sensible with the 'lots of drinks' advice, you do not want to cause your child any physical harm.** That is, don't force the drinks down, let him drink freely – this is why, as suggested earlier in this chapter, you may need to forgo your rules about no fizzy drinks or juices so he is more than happy to drink lots of his favourites, just until we get this toileting under control.

Strategy Three – Fixed Scheduling

This is maybe the most energy draining of the three strategies suggested in this book. However, if you feel the other two strategies are unlikely to be suitable for your child, or what you can realistically cope with, this may be the one to try. It may also be an option if you have given one or both the others a try, and had little to no success

Step One

Set a day or two aside where you will have little to no interruption in regards to appointments, etc. You need to decide on a set timeframe for taking your child to the toilet for the first part of this strategy. That is, every 20 minutes, 30 minutes, or 40 minutes? We suggest 20, but definitely no more than 40 minutes between toilet trips. One thing you need to take into consideration around this is how often your child usually wets or poos in her nappy, if it is very regular, the shorter time span of 20 minutes would be better, if it is only 2 – 3 times per day, the 40 minutes may be the better option. Either way, the whole goal of this strategy is to get your child into the habit of going to the toilet from whatever room they are in, and to interrupt whatever it is she is doing to go to the toilet instead of going in her nappy.

Step Two

At the time you have decided on (lets say you start the exercise at 9am, and decided on 20 minute intervals) pick your child up, simply say "toilet time" and have no other interaction with her. Once in the toilet, remove the nappy and place her on the toilet seat. Stay with her there for at least four minutes (this doesn't sound that long, but it will seem like a lifetime once you start this exercise!). If she gets off the toilet, simply place her back on as gently and calmly as you can, not having any other verbal interaction with her. At the end of the four minutes, get her off the toilet, say "Good girl" (or boy - accordingly) put her nappy back on, and let her make her own way back to what she was doing. If she voids while on the toilet seat, ensure you immediately provide her with lots of verbal reinforcement -

"Great, fantastic, what a good girl, well done, you did wee/poo in the toilet - that's so good"! Give her a hug, and then finish the process - wiping and flushing (let her help with this if possible – but do not force her). Now also provide a special reinforcer, this may be a special video or music CD, favourite game, etc (as discussed earlier in this chapter). It is important you provide this special reinforcer immediately after the success, to connect the special 'treat' with the good appropriate behaviour.

Step Three

Continue as above. When/if you have success with her voiding in the toilet bowl twice, now try her with just undies on – loose the nappy. Also now change from carrying her to the toilet, to leading her by her hand.

Step Four

After another two successes, instead of leading her by her hand, just use the verbal prompt of "Toilet time", and walk there with her.

Step Five

After one more success, now increase your time spans by 10 minutes, but obviously if your child prompts you that she needs to go – by either making her way there by herself, or saying "Toilet time" go with her at that time, do not try and wait until the time period is up.

Now simply let things take their course. That is, slowly increase the time spans (little by little) until you feel comfortable she can/does now go to the toilet under her own steam, or prompts you to let you know she needs to go. Guard against her becoming reliant on you always accompanying her, start going only to the toilet door, then to just before the toilet door, and so on until she is comfortable going the whole way by herself. Again remember to generalise and have your partner or other caregivers take turns in following through the strategy. If you have more than one toilet at home, alternate between them so she is not reliant on just one toilet for going in, and will help her to adjust to using toilets in other environments.

WHAT IF ...

'She keeps weeing in her nappy, and after a whole day of following this strategy we have had no successes at all?'

That's ok! But what it does mean is that you need to repeat the process again the next day, and maybe the next – until you get those successes!. Until you get that first, and often second success, your child may not understand what it is they are supposed to be doing on the toilet, nor will they experience the positive reinforcers that you are going to provide once she does void in the toilet. So, to help with this, on day two now provide a drink five minutes before the time period ends. That is, if you are using 20 minute time periods (and you should be using the shorter ones now if you had no success with longer time spans) then provide a drink after about 15 minutes. Also, increase the time sitting on the toilet to six minutes.

'If still no successes?"

If still no successes after two (by now very tiring) days, have a one-day break. When trying the third day, follow the suggestions as above, but this time keep her on the toilet until she does void. Have a book or toy there she can play with to help pass the time, and lessen the chances of boredom and resulting tantrums.

'We had two successes, but now I have tried her with underwear she is getting really upset and refusing to wear them, she wants the nappies back even though she is weeing in the loo'

Go back to nappies, and keep up with the strategy as outlined, just pass on the undies stage at the moment. Once you feel she is having more successes than wet/dirty nappies, now start a desensitisation process for wearing undies as outlined at the end of this chapter.

Night Time TIPs

The biggest factor in achieving night time success (that is, either a dry night, or your child waking and appropriately toileting with little to no support) is firstly achieving day time success. That is, when they are using the toilet with little to no prompting during the day, the night time with eventually come right.

However, sometimes nights do become yet another obstacle to overcome in the toilet training drama! So, here are some tips that may make things a little easier:

- **The Basics:** There are some very basic things that will help with nights. Firstly, no drinks within 90 minutes of bedtime. Always ensure they go to toilet within ten minutes of going to bed. Do NOT put any pressure on them to "have a dry night". If you make a big fuss about this, they will worry all night long – stress will increase the likelihood of them wetting the bed. When there is an 'accident' (a wet bed) again, do NOT make a fuss about it. Do not tell them off, do not tell them you are sad about it, nothing. Instead just clean it up in a low key manner.

- **Trial Runs:** On the first night of trying the night time strategy, you will start by playing a game. Once it is early evening and just starting to get dark, go to your child's bedroom with them. Tell them you are going to play a game, you will say "When I say toilet time, you have to go straight to the toilet from here, and you have to beat me there. But, no running". You will of course, let them get there first – in fact stay at least two metres behind them so they get used to the idea of walking to the toilet from their room at night. When you get there behind them, let your child know how happy you are they won. Give them a special reinforcer right then. Now repeat this at least twice more. You can do this each night for the first three nights.

> **One Step at a Time – Night Toileting Strategy:** Remember this 'toilet thing' is a new experience, and just learning the daytime routine has been a big trial for your child. So when it comes to night-time toileting don't expect miracles the first night. On the first night, do put your child to bed in underwear rather than a nappy. However, you are going to wake them up after three hours, and prompt them to go to the toilet. Yes, they will be grumpy and you will be in the bad books. Once they get to the toilet, ensure they sit on the bowl for at least a minute – even if they do not void. Do not keep them much longer than a minute though – again we do not want to make the toileting experience a bad one. When they get back to their room, you can put their nappy back on for the night (If you want to try the rest of the night in undies, that is fine too – but again, do not expect a miracle). Repeat this three more nights, and then the next three stretch it out to three and a half hours before toileting. What you have now achieved is your child is used to going to bed in undies and

getting up to go toilet from their bed. You can now attempt the first night in undies

- **There are products to help:** Unfortunately it is likely you will have some wet beds, and you will cringe at the thought of yet more bedclothes to wash! But there are some products that will help you get through this faze. You can get plastic or rubber under-sheets that stop the moisture soaking through into the mattress.

WHAT IF ...

"I have tried and tried what you have suggested, but she still keeps wetting her nappy at night time". Again look at how much your child is drinking leading up to bedtime. Remember, no drinks within 90 minutes of bedtime, and before this, frequent small drinks would be better than two or three large ones.

"I've done that, but still wet nappies"! Ok. You will need to do the long yards I'm afraid. Night one – put your child to bed in undies, as the original strategy advises. Wake her after two hours, toilet. Wake her another two hours, toilet. Then three hours time, toilet. That should be enough for the night. Repeat this for one more night. The third night, wake her every three hours for toileting. Next night, wake once after three hours, leave her in nappies. Keep this up for at least another three or four nights. Now, again try for a full night – in undies. If still no success (or at least if no more successes than failures), then seek medical advice as your child may possibly have a bladder problem. This may not be the case, but always check it out. If there is no medical problem, again go back to trying the original strategy, remembering all the 'basic tips'.

"The biggest factor in achieving night time success is firstly achieving day time success"

POO'S IN THE LOO

ROUTINE and HABIT

Passing bowel motions usually follows a specific routine in regards to when the bowel motion occurs. This routine becomes more regular with age, and is not quite so regular when we are very young. However, you should find that your child often does have a bowel motion (BM) during a certain time period of the day or night. This might be between 9am and 11am, or 6pm and 8pm. Whenever it is, you need to be watching your child extra closely so you can pick up any signs that they may be about to have a BM, so the next time they show those signs you can take them straight to the toilet and sit them on it hopefully to get them to have the BM then and there. The more they associate that feeling of about to have a bowel motion and then sitting on the toilet, the more likely they will start doing this without your prompts.

WHAT DOES IT FEEL LIKE WHEN I NEED TO 'POO'?

One issue with BM's is that they feel different from having a 'wee'. That is, the physical sensations that your child now recognises as meaning they need to wee are different from those for when they need to 'poo'. When you can get that first BM in the toilet, you are on your way to getting more BMs in there. Just like the weeing, as your child learns to associate the physical sensations of having a full bowel with sitting on the toilet, they will start to self-initiate that behaviour.

ISN'T THAT WHAT NAPPIES ARE FOR?

Many parents keep using nappies even though their child has now mastered the urination side of toileting, in case they 'have an accident'. But to a child, the fact they are still wearing nappies may be a little confusing. In other words, now that they wee in the toilet, why do they still have this nappy thing on? Maybe because that is what you do your poos in?

You will need to try and get out of the habit of using nappies (including 'Pull Ups') as soon as possible after your child has mainly successes with 'weeing' in the toilet. Though you may still want a nappy on occasions if you are going out somewhere and they still have the odd accident, at home try to be completely nappy-free. This in itself will help aid your child to understand that everything that comes out below belongs only in the loo.

GAMES ARE GOOD

Believe it or not, doing poos is not a fun experience for some kids. All that pushing while sitting over a big hole can be scary. Bowel motions can also cause some discomfort and even pain, so the thought of sitting on the toilet doing the poos can be daunting to a small child.

To help ease some of this possible anxiety, make a game out of 'poo's in the loo'.

For example, have a colour-in picture on the toilet wall. Each time your child does do a poo in the loo they get to colour in a part of the picture. When the picture is all coloured in, they get a 'prize'. Of course again you want to reinforce the BM in the toilet behaviour straight away, and make it quick and easy to get the reinforcement. So, especially the first two or three times they get their BM in the toilet, give them a special treat straight away. Remember to also tell them how happy and pleased you are with them.

DON'T PUNISH FOR ACCIDENTS

If you growl your child when they do have a BM in their nappy or pants (or dare I say it – somewhere else), don't be angry with them. In fact don't make a fuss one way or the other. Simply clean it up, don't say anything about what happened, and once all is cleaned up – you can simply say (in a non sarcastic manner) "Never mind, next time we will get the 'poo in the loo'."

If you tell them off, or make them feel unhappy or uncomfortable about what happened, next time they may be even more secretive about it, not wanting you to know. They may even associate the act of having a BM as being bad altogether, and so even going to the toilet won't be an option, because 'Mum will know and I'll get told off again'.

DESENSITISATION

- **Mummy, I really don't like wearing undies!**

Some children have difficulty going from nappies to undies. This is particularly common with children who have autism, and also seen with some other developmentally delayed children. Don't get distressed about this, there is a solution.

Below are some simple guidelines for desensitising your child to wearing undies:

1) **Get them involved in the undies choosing exercise!** That is, when you go out to buy some, take them with you – let them select the colour/pattern that they like. At this stage you do not want to frighten or stress them, so you do not need to even say things like "These are what you will be wearing", simply say, something like "Look at these pretty pants – which ones do you think are the nicest?". Yes, it's true that some children will still be too young to have much input here, and in some cases you may have already bought the undies, or your child may not be at a level where they can participate in this sort of exercise. However, where possible, do follow this step prior to implementing the toilet training.

2) **Don't just shove them straight on.** Going from wearing the same thing day after day all your life (well your life to date at 2 years or so of age) to something that looks different, feels different, and is all about NOT weeing or pooing in, can

naturally be frightening or at least stressful for many children. What you need to do is let them get used to the idea, slowly. This is what we call desensitising.

3) **Let your child get used to what they look like.** Let them get used to what they look like. Leave them on a chair or on the dresser in their room for a day or two.

4) **Let him see what they are like to touch.** Remember, this is a different type of material from what they are used to having against their skin. Create opportunities where they can pick them up, and hold them. Play a game where you sit the undies on their knee, see how well they can fold them up, and so on. Anything that involves them getting used to the feel of them is great.

The process of following the above steps may take a few days to implement, particularly if your child is reacting in a negative way to the wearing of underpants. If the process is not helped by following the basic suggestions above, you should read the chapter on desensitisation and design a specific program to follow to get over this obstacle.

- **No Way am I sitting on That Seat with the Big Hole in it!**

Some children are terrified of toilets right from the start! They are worried about falling through the hole, the seat is freezing cold, they feel insecure, the toilet is small and frightening, or it's just that it is something so different to everything else they do. To help combat your child's fear of sitting on the toilet, you may need to desensitise them to the experience before embarking on the strategies of toilet training.

1) **Get them used to the toilet area.** Play the odd game outside the toilet area, in the hallway. Have the toilet door open, occasionally let a ball or toy roll in there so your child needs to go in there and retrieve it. (yes hygiene is a concern, but I am sure you will have mopped and cleaned in there before going to this step!).

2) **Ensure the toilet is a nice place to visit.** Is it clean? Does it smell nice? Buy a poster or two that your child will love to look at, involve them in the process of sticking these on the toilet walls (blue tack will do nicely here). Have them positioned so you actually need to enter the toilet room to see them properly. Ensure there is an air freshener or similar there. Maybe a novelty ornament on the windowsill may also be helpful.

3) **Get them used to the sensation of sitting on a seat with a hole.** There are a few ways you can achieve this. One, if you see a cheap toilet seat for sale – great, buy it! Then play a game where the toilet seat sits on the sofa or another chair, and your child has to sit on the seat (ensure this is a fun exercise though, don't frighten them with the seat!). As there is no gapping hole at this time, they shouldn't have too much of a concern about it. If you have an old plastic chair (like the plastic garden chairs), carefully cut out a small hole in the

middle of the seat area (only about 5 cm's wide at this stage), encourage your child to sit on this seat, again use it as part of a game, or when they have their lunch maybe this is the chair they sit on – just for now. Each day, for the next five days, cut about an extra centimeter around the hole, so by the fifth day the hole is now around 10cms across. Have them sit on the seat say two more times, before going into the toilet training strategy.

If the process is not helped by following the basic suggestions above, you should read the specific chapter on desensitisation in this book.

AUTISM AND TOILET TRAINING

Below we cover some issues you need to keep in mind when going through the toilet training process with a child who has autism. You may find my chapter on Autism in this book is also helpful when toilet training a child with autism.

Firstly, some children with autism may not have any problem with toilet training at all, in fact some may even toilet train faster than typically developed children. However, many others do have extra difficulties with toileting, and often the reasons may relate to some of the issues outlined below. Also, it is not uncommon for a child with autism to be around four or even five years of age before Parents start tackling the toileting issue, so do not feel guilty or isolated if your child is around this age.

> **Loss of routine:** Many children with autism live there lives via routines that they have formed, or adjusted to. So, changing from voiding in a nappy, to now being expected to sit on a plastic or wooden seat with a hole in it, is a frightening experience. Often the routines they have developed have given them a sense of control over what is otherwise a chaotic and frightening World full of movements, noises, colours and smells. For this reason, using desensitisation methods, as suggested earlier, and getting tem used to the changes more slowly may help. This doe not mean you can not use the strategies listed here, it just means some extra work beforehand may be needed. In fact studies

trialing strategies similar to ours, have shown that even severely autistic children can be toilet trained within days.

> **Concrete Thinking:** If it is black and white, it is black and white – not white and black! This type of thinking is common in autism. What you see, is what it is. So, if I poo in the toilet bowl, I need to know this is what is supposed to happen to my poos. That is, we need to make it clear that this behaviour is correct, good, and positive. Ensure they see others in the household using the toilet, let them watch a member of the same sex go through the whole process (yes a little uncomfortable for some I know, but it may be very helpful particularly for some with autism). However, empathic understanding lacks in most with autism. That is, they have difficulty seeing others points of view – or even understanding that others have feelings, and so just because someone else does their poos and wees in the toilet, doesn't mean I do! So – using visuals may help overcome this issue. What we would recommend is having their photo, at the top of a card, followed by sketches of a person weeing and pooing ('boardmaker' type visuals may be useful here), then a photo of your toilet bowl, all with a smiley face or tick next to them. Again, our chapter on autism may has more details on use of visuals and training your child to understand them. Depending on your child's current level of understanding (their level of intellectual disability) let them know the 'rule is, all wees and poos go in the toilet'. You may need to repeat this 'rule' dozens of times over a period of weeks to really get

the message across, but once they have understood and accepted this rule, you will find in almost all cases they stick to it like glue!

> **What happens, how does it work?** With autism comes what could be termed, a natural curiosity of how things work. This may be related to their need to have some sort of control over the chaotic World around them. So, talking about (and using pictures) of 'where your poos go' once they are flushed, may be helpful. Show a picture of the toilet bowl, the pipe going from the toilet bowl to the main sew pipe, and some sort of representation of the sewerage plant. Show, and explain, how their poos in the toilet go down the pipe, into the big pipe, and to the sewer where they turn to dirt (or whatever more imaginative description you can come up with). Though some affected by autism are effected to such an extent they may not be able to understand these concepts, others who can may find this very helpful.

> **Generalise:** As people with autism are very rule based in their behaviour, governed by routine and structure, you need to be extra careful about generalising what is being taught. In other words, introduce other toilets in other environments early in the training process. Use other support people and family members in the training. Differ times, clothing worn, and route you take to the toilet (where applicable) so your child does not just toilet appropriately for one person, or only in one environment, or only during the daytime or evening,

etc. If you stick to a specific routine (same person, same training times, etc) you may well find they will also stick to these, as this has become the set toileting routine.

Important Toilet Training Note

The strategies listed above, are fairly general and non-specific to any one individual. Some children, particularly those who display very challenging behaviour or have a severe to profound intellectual or developmental disability may require a custom designed toilet training strategy, or the assistance of trained therapists. However, we recommend you trial the strategies as outlined above, and do not give up easily, as they have been successful in training even severely intellectually disabled children in a relatively sort period of time.

The author does not make any guarantees that the strategies will be successful, nor can we take responsibility for any unwanted results. Though the author has used specialist knowledge in designing these strategies, those who follow them take all care and responsibility themselves for all and any outcome.

ANGER MANAGEMENT
The Dior Method

This chapter has been written in a way that it can be utilised by either the person with the anger management issue, or by someone supporting them. It has been written in a way that will guide you to write down, understand and follow your own anger management strategy. Or, to guide you writing an anger management strategy that will help you with your support of the person who needs the strategy.

Anger Management is maybe the one issue that if perfected by us all, could well cut our violent crime rate by up to 90%, or at the very least would lessen the impact of domestic and schoolyard problems.

Understanding Anger
Anger is *not* a bad emotion. Many people do not realise this, and view anger as something we should never have, yet it is simply another 'emotion', which we have for a reason. Emotions tell us and often others around us, that something is not quite right, and we need to do something to change the situation. The feeling of anger puts across one of many messages. Firstly, it tells us that something has happened or is happening that is either not safe or not fair to what we believe should be happening. It also tells us that we need to do

something to either stop what is happening, or to remove ourselves from the situation.

I base what I teach in this anger management chapter on what I term the **Dior Method**. What the **Dior Method** refers to is scientifically based strategies that are based on behavioural principles. This means I base the advice I provide on what can be observed by others, either visually (what we see happen), what we hear, smell, or feel. Subsequently we need to base our understanding of anger on these principles, rather than just the emotive descriptions of anger ('hate, vengeance, despise').

Like all behaviours, what we do when we are angry serves a function for us. For example, if we hit a person when we are angry with what they have just said – the function of this behaviour is to either stop them from saying what they are saying, or to reduce the likelihood they will say these things again as we have just inflicted a punishment on them. We obviously need to work on modifying this behaviour, and to do that successfully we need to introduce an appropriate behaviour to take its place that fulfils the same function.

"The feeling of anger puts across one of many messages"

Life is about rules. If we break those rules, more often than not we will face the consequences, and regret that we did break them. We need our own set of rules to get through life without getting ourselves either into jail, or into a fight where we get hurt.

The last three opening paragraphs you read have introduced the three main steps of the *Dior Method* anger management strategy. Those three steps are:

Knowing what our body feels like and what we do when we get angry

Having a plan about what we will do in future when our body feels like that

Having our own personal rules that relate to our anger that we will endeavor to never break

As this chapter progresses, we go through each of these three steps, explaining how you can work out the best way to follow them and subsequently form them into your own strategy. The reasoning behind you writing your own strategy is all related to how we all react to the emotion of anger differently. Where some of us who are constantly teased or verbally bullied by others may simply react by walking away and ignoring it, others will react with violence. Yet, there are also many other reactions that may be shown by many other people in exactly the same situation. This is why different things will work for each of us in controlling our anger. **Though we provide examples and suggestions, only YOU can decide on what will work for you.**

A person who wants to learn a strategy to stop smoking, is wasting their time unless they actually **WANT TO STOP**. Anger management is exactly the same. *Unless you WANT to stop reacting as you do at the moment, it is no use learning strategies.*

So, why is it you need anger management strategies?

- **For yourself, to reduce the chance of Police involvement?**

- **To help someone else with anger management problems?**

- **To stop your friends or family from getting hurt?**

- **Because you know you will, or have hurt someone – physically, or mentally?**

Whatever your reason is for taking the Anger Management Course in this book, before you progress through the rest of the information you need to read and understand the next section – Anger is not the problem.

Anger – is NOT the Problem

Feeling angry does not harm other people. Feeling annoyed, will not hurt anyone. In fact, there is no emotion that will do any damage to anything or anyone. However, what we do while experiencing that emotion is what can damage others or you.

Yes, your ACTIONS are the problem, not your anger itself. That is, you don't need to change how you feel, but you do need to change how you respond.

However, there are some things that will help to tone down that feeling of 'rage' which leads to behaviour that some of us find so hard to control.

Look for Humour in the Situation: If someone is giving you some verbal abuse, try putting their words into pictures. So – the abusive words *"You Pig",* turns into a picture of a large pink pig rolling around in mud, with a human face smiling away in delight. You may also find humour in seeing how the other person is starting to 'lose it', while you think about how you can just walk away before you get to the stage they have reached.

Situational Test Runs and Relaxation: If there are specific situations that get you angry on a regular basis, and you know one of those situations is coming up, do a 'test run' before you actually go through the real situation. This is one of the few times in this entire book we refer to the use of imagination. Firstly, ensure you are standing up - now tense all your muscles *(make tight fists, curl those toes, get into a body builder type pose – showing off those muscles).* Now imagine you are walking into that anger inducing situation right now – *that relative who is always sarcastic, that workmate who leaves all the hard work to you, that guy who steals your prize veggies from the garden, those kids who tease you at lunchtime, or whatever it is.* Think about what it is they are likely to say or do, while you think about this, slowly relax your muscles. It is important you do this slowly (over at least one to two minutes) while you still imagine those comments or actions that usually make you feel *so angry!* Once you have relaxed all your muscles sit down and rest, and as you do this you should now stop imagining the anger inducing situation, and rest for a few minutes – congratulating yourself on being calm. You need to repeat this at least two more times. Try it again the next day, again with two repeats.

Believe it or Not, the Whole World is *NOT* Against *You*: It is very important you realise that many of the situations that you get involved in each week that may often result in you becoming angry, happen to millions of other people as well. If they can handle these situations calmly, then hey – guess what – so can YOU! However, this all sounds very easy, and as you would well know by now though you can understand this point, the situations still make you feel full of rage. The strategy you are about to construct, following our advice and examples, will help you cope with this, but you must also work on that 'mindset' of yours – **keep telling yourself, "The World is NOT against me".**

"Your ACTIONS are the problem, not the anger itself"

Exactly What Do You Do when You Are Angry?

We need to establish what it is we do when we are feeling angry, and how our body feels. Many people I have worked with around anger management say that often their anger happens so quickly that they hit out, then realize what they have done afterwards and regret their actions. Few of us can claim to have never had that same experience, maybe not to the degree of hitting another person, but certainly saying or doing something because we were angry and then regretting it afterwards.

Another common comment about anger is *"I just get so angry – I just can't stop myself!"* Like other emotions, anger plays an important role in our life, yet for many of us it does not rule our life, for others it may do. The main difference here is that most of us know when we are getting angry, and do something before we get to the **point of no return,** others with anger problems struggle to identify the point of no return and often end up with what can be described as **uncontrollable rage.**

Imagine for a moment you are on a skateboard, you are at the top of a very steep road, and plan on attempting to skate down this road. Near the bottom there are people everywhere, and the road surface gets very rough. You know that to have any chance of successfully getting down at least some of the road, you need a plan. That plan includes judging how fast you are getting up to on your board, and being able to jump off at that stage and grab your board before you get to such a speed that the only thing that can happen is disaster.

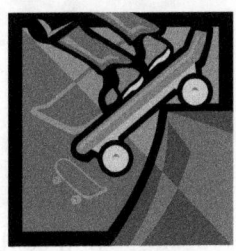

If you stay on the board, you will get so fast that stopping is impossible (the point of no return), and you will soon hit the rough surface at such a speed you are bound to fall off hurting yourself, and others.

Anger, is very much the same. It starts off as a slow *in control* ride, but very quickly things start getting *out of control*.

We need to know when we are in those first stages of anger, so we know to follow our very first step of anger management (knowing when to 'get off the board'), which is to:

STOP

The way we do this, is to recognize how our body feels, because this knowledge is what we will use to tell us we need to 'jump off that board now', get over to the side and get back in control. That is, when our body feels this way, **we need to stop what we are saying and doing**, and get away from the situation or use one of the other strategies that we will discuss later on.

So, how does your body feel when you are angry?

- Do you feel hot?
- Feel full of hot air?
- Do your fists clench up?
- Do you start to raise your voice, begin to shout?
- Does your breathing get faster?
- Start pacing back and forth?
- Begin to stutter?

- ➤ Eyes widen, start staring at others eye to eye?
- ➤ Slap your sides with your hands?
- ➤ Roll your eyes?

It may be other things, but you *need to identify what it is you do when you get angry.*
These are your warning signs, and your body's way of saying "Hey, I need to get out of here"! *This* - may very well be that point of no return, if you do not act when you feel those physical warning signs, it may be very hard, if not near impossible, to stop the escalation of your anger to the stage where someone gets hurt. You need to put a STOP to that escalation right then and there. Now you have stopped what you were saying and doing, what now?

The next step of your anger strategy is to:

WALK AWAY

You need to walk away

To help you walk away from the situation, you need to first stop that escalation of anger so you can think clear enough to be able to walk away. That is why you need to start memorizing your steps of YOUR strategy – **STOP - WALK AWAY**. Remember, anger happens very quickly, and unless your reactions are as quick as your temper – you are always going to be in trouble!

The things to keep in mind about the 'walk away' step are:

- Go somewhere quiet
- If possible, go somewhere where you can be alone

> Try and be in a location where you can not hear or see the person or event that was making you feel that way

At the end of this chapter you will find a page for you to start writing in your own anger management strategy.

The first part of your strategy is printed already – that is STOP. The next is WALK AWAY.

The next section is for you to write your early warning signs in, so as above -, think about what it is you do/feel (physically) when you start becoming angry, then write these in the space provided.

"Remember, anger happens very quickly, and unless your reactions are as quick as your temper – you are always going to be in trouble"

Stop, Walk Away, But Then What?
Most of us know the most common advice about what to do when we are angry, that is "Walk Away". Just like a steaming pot of water, removing it from the source that is heating it up is a good start to see some cooling down begin, and the same goes with walking away

from who or what is making you so angry. But, again like the steaming pot of water, you are going to remain 'hot' for some time. While you are in this state, the chance that you will still do something unacceptable is high. In other words, you need to do something to help you 'calm down'.

Once you have walked away, think about things you enjoy doing that preferably involve some sort of physical movement. That is, if you can do something that helps burn off some of that extra energy you have during that time of cooling down; it will help speed up the process.

Here are some ideas of things you can do to help calm down:

- ➤ **Go for a jog or running on the spot**
- ➤ **Go for a long walk, or a shorter up-hill walk**
- ➤ **Push ups or sit ups**
- ➤ **Drawing (the faster, like 'speed sketching', the better)**
- ➤ **Ripping up scrap paper**
- ➤ **Lifting weights (even milk bottles full of water will do)**
- ➤ **Pull some weeds out of the garden**

If physical activities like these are not possible, due to a disability or other reasons, try other activities that you usually enjoy, these will refocus you on to other things and help that calming process.

Here are some suggestions – but only you know what you like and what you do not.

- Looking through magazines
- Fairly loud, but calming, music through earplugs (classical, instrumental, ballads, - NOT heavy rock or RAP)
- Reading a book
- Surfing the internet
- Folding laundry, or even origami or weaving

Some will say that when you are at this stage, still feeling 'full of anger', that doing relaxing type activities like reading a book is just not an option. But this is incorrect. **The way to reduce that anger is to refocus onto matters that were not the original cause of your anger.**

I do NOT recommend 'punch bags'. Many so-called 'anger management counselors' often tell the people they are working with or their support people, to purchase a punch bag (sometimes called a boxing bag). I strongly recommend you do *not* do this. Connecting the sensations of anger with going and hitting something, well, it is common sense really what the possible eventual consequences may be. What happens when you are out, or staying away from home and you do not have that bag, what (who?) do you hit then? This is why instead I suggest you learn to do other activities that you can do almost anywhere.

Now you have thought about the type of things you can do after you have walked away, write them down on the next section of your anger management strategy ('Then I need to ...... to calm down').

Your basic anger management strategy is now:

STOP

WALK AWAY

CALM DOWN

You now need to back up this strategy with rules that will become a very important part of your life that is if you are <u>serious</u> about controlling your anger.

Rules for Life - Rules for Anger

Many people who get themselves in trouble because of their anger, struggle with accepting what they do when they are angry, or what they have done in the past, was not ok. We have probably all heard the excuse *"Yeah, I hit him, but he deserved it – anyone else would have done the same, he was asking for it"*. It's like they are rationalizing their behaviour, saying it was 'ok' because they were angry and the rules are different then.

In fact, it is quite the opposite. We need extra rules that we must follow when we are angry. Though you may add other rules to your anger management strategy, we strongly suggest the following three are 'core rules' for when you are angry. No Hitting. No Threatening. No Swearing. They seem obvious, and they are, yet they are the three things that can cause the most damage – to others and to you in regards of possible consequences.

The only way to remember any rule is by repetition. How did you learn the road rules? By repetition, reading them over and over. How did you learn grammatical rules for writing? By repetition, practicing them over and over. I'm afraid; you have to 'go the long yards' here as well. You need to repeat your anger rules over and over, we suggest five times each night as soon as you get into bed, and five times on waking. It is important you have set times (or better still – specific cues that alert you to now recite the rules) or you will simply forget; in this case bed and waking are the cues.

Some may say the 'no swearing' rule is a little "precious", and why should they follow that anger rule? The reason we strongly suggest that rule is one of your three core rules is because often swearing is the beginning of a very fast escalation in anger. In other words, as soon as you let the 'abuse fly' remembering the STOP, WALK AWAY, and CALM DOWN strategy may be very hard to do. Swearing at anyone, especially in anger, is also often a trigger to make them angry, and possibly retaliate with violence as they take offence to what you have said.

Now think of up to two other anger rules you need to follow. You may determine these by thinking about what you have done in the past that has hurt others, and you know it was simply unacceptable. This may be, putting someone down, making personal comments about someone's looks, throwing objects, breaking things, etc.

NO HITTING

NO THREATENING

NO SWEARING

Now write in the space provided on your strategy the two rules you have thought of.

If This Is YOUR Strategy
You need to go through your strategy each morning, straight after dressing for the day, or straight after breakfast and again just before getting into bed at night. Read it from beginning to end, as you read it think about how this well help prevent you from harming others, or yourself. Read it through twice on each occasion.

Place the strategy on your bedroom wall where you can't help but see it every time you go into your bedroom. You need to be reminded of it as much as possible, you **MUST** read it as we have suggested above. If not, anger will catch you by surprise, you won't remember quickly enough what you are supposed to do, and you may regret what you end up doing yet again!

Think of the positives of going through this process. You will be proud of yourself; you are going from *little control* to *better control* of yourself. Others will notice how you improve, they too will become proud of what you achieve, and they will notice that you are taking back control of your anger rather than your anger controlling you.

YOU CAN DO THIS, YOU NEED TO DO THIS – ITS SIMPLE, BUT IT'S HARD WORK, YOU NEED TO FOLLOW WHAT WE HAVE SUGGESTED IF YOU WANT SUCCESS, BUT YOU CAN DO IT!

If You Are Supporting Someone Else With This Strategy
Read it to them each night, and each morning. Talk about each step - how can they remember each step? Why is the strategy important? How can you help them remember the steps and rules?

Let them know you are proud of them for wanting to take control of their anger. Praise them for each success; tell them how great they are doing. Don't put them down if they forget the strategy, and have a 'slip up'. Instead, tell them 'not to worry, we can go through your strategy again, and you WILL remember next time'.

"Connecting the sensations of anger with going and hitting something, well, it is common sense really what the possible eventual consequences may be"

Last Helpful Hints on Anger Management
When you are out and about, each time you pass a STOP sign think to yourself *"Yes, that's me, I Stop when getting angry, I walk away and I calm down"*. The stop signs are your special cues, and will help you remember to follow your strategy.

What about when you can't walk away? There are times when walking away is not an option. For example when you are sitting in a vehicle and someone does something that makes you feel those warning signs, yet you can not just get up and walk out. So, instead – always remember the first step 'Stop' – now distract your mind from what is going on. *If in a vehicle look out the window, concentrate on what is passing – play a game in your own mind, count how many red cars pass, or how many busses, etc.* If there is music playing, focus intensely on that, listen for the different instruments, think about the words being sung, etc. The key thing here is to focus your mind on something else, rather than letting those words or actions that are making you angry take over all your senses and elevate that anger level to the 'point of no return'.

Anger IS About YOU: So often people blame their anger, and more accurately what they did when they were angry, on everyone else. *'It was his fault. They shouldn't have done that. They made me angry. You always wind me up.'* **You have to accept that only YOU are responsible for what you do when you are angry.** Subsequently, only YOU can choose to follow your new anger management strategy. Only YOU will determine whether you take back control of your anger, or whether you continue to let it take control of your life. Stop blaming others, and work hard on memorising your strategy, memorizing your anger rules – you can do this, if you choose to. If you are supporting someone else with this strategy, you can help them take control by going over the strategy with them time and time again, and prompting them when they get angry *"Remember what you need to do, stop, walk away, and go and do something to calm down".*

"Yes, that's me, I Stop when getting angry, I walk away and I calm down"

"Only YOU will determine whether you take back control of your anger or whether you continue to let it take control of your life"

My Anger Management Strategy

I know when I am getting angry because my body feels like this

_____

, and I start doing the following things:

_____

_____

This is when I need to STOP what I am saying and doing

I then need to **WALK AWAY**

        AND THEN I NEED TO:

        _____

        _____

        _____

        To help me **CALM DOWN**

My Anger Rules which I must never break are:

NO Hitting, NO Threatening, NO Swearing and

_____

Remembering my strategy and my anger rules means I will stay: *Out of trouble*, **and** *in control of my future*

Solving Sleep Problems With Children

***If there is* one issue that affects a whole family, especially the Parents, it is when a child has a sleeping problem.** Not only does the child not get enough sleep, which can impact on their mood, behaviour, energy, and level of motivation, but the Parent/s often start missing out on their sleep too. It is because of this that as a Behaviour Specialist, I will often try and get any sleep issues under control as much as possible before targeting other challenging behaviours. With a tired child, and tired Parents, trying to modify other behaviours is going to be very difficult.

There are three different categories that the majority of sleep problems fall into. Yet, no matter which category the problem falls into, most can be addressed with the same type of strategies, with the odd exception. Subsequently the "Dior Method" strategy is supplied for addressing these categories of sleep problems.

1) Not wanting to go to bed/sleep

These are the children who may tantrum when told it's bedtime, and drag their official bed time way past when it is supposed to be. Or, they lay in bed not being able to fall asleep, or constantly playing with toys instead of getting to sleep.

These problems usually relate to routines, or lack of them. But they can also be due to the child simply not needing the amount of sleep that the Parents think they need. Further in this chapter I list the average amounts of sleep that children need according to their age.

2) Not staying asleep or in bed / Early morning waking

This category includes the children that wake often during the night, or wake very early in the morning and don't go back to sleep again. Waking during the night can be due to a few different factors. The child may need to use the toilet, they have a wet or dirty nappy, or are what is often called a "light sleeper" and so are easily woken by noises, or they do not feel secure in their bedroom (afraid of the dark, or are a long way from the Parents bedroom).

Children who wake then can't get back to sleep, may face the same issue as some of the children in the first category, in that they don't need as much sleep as their Parents think they do. This is sometimes easily fixed by simply making their bedtime a little later, and making sure they get enough exercise each day.

This category also includes those children who may shout out, cry, or continually come to their parent's or other family member's beds during the night. This is specifically addressed in the 'Night Time Criers' section later in this chapter.

3) Wanting to sleep elsewhere other than in their own bed

This one is quite a common issue, especially in the under five year old age group, but can also affect older children. Usually the child wants to sleep in the Parent's bed, rather than in their own (sometimes termed 'Co-sleeping').

This issue, a little like the first, is often around routine, in that they have been allowed to sleep in the Parents bed once or twice, maybe because they were sick, and so simply want this to continue. It can also be due to the child feeling insecure, in that they are frightened to sleep in their own room, or maybe are just uncomfortable in their own room/bed.

Unfortunately though Mum, and Dad or Caregivers, in most cases you are a lot to blame for this problem. Many Parents simply decide that putting little Johnny or Sally back to bed when they have climbed into theirs is too much of a bother. They are tired, and it is so much easier to just let them sleep in your bed, "just this one time though."

The 'Dior Method' – For Getting Them to Bed, and to Sleep

(For category 1 problems, and as a basis for the other two categories of sleep problems)

This first strategy, 'The Dior Method', incorporates suggestions that should help address almost any of the sleep problems that fall into one of the three categories already outlined, but in particular may be all you need for those children who just have difficulty in getting to bed, and getting to sleep. Like other issues addressed by 'The Dior Method', these strategies are based on the principles of Applied Behaviour Analysis but also incorporate some other methods that I have also used successfully in my work as a Behaviour Specialist.

Important Notes for Pre-Bedtime
It is best if only low stimuli activities occur in the hour before bed time, that is: reading, writing, drawing, and even watching TV (as long as it's not a scary movie, or the news) are all good, running around, play fighting or playing hide and seek or similar is not.

Try and avoid ALL foods and (with the exception below) all drinks for the 90 minutes before bedtime. In fact, if you can stretch that to two hours, even better. Though some sleep experts disagree, personally I think a small glass of water or milk about 30 minutes before bed is usually ok and will stave off thirst or bedtime 'hunger feelings', as long as you ensure they go to toilet immediately before bedtime. If your child has problems with night time enuresis (bed wetting), firstly read the chapter on toilet training in the book 'Behaviour Skills for Parents and Support People' by Trevor Lewis for suggestions to combat that, and secondly (for these children) avoid ALL drinks within 90 minutes of bedtime.

You may be surprised to hear that adults (especially if trying to lose weight) should avoid all food and drink for 4 to 5 hours before bedtime!
The good old hot chocolate or hot Milo, is not a good idea. Though it is a pleasant way to finish a day before bed, the majority of people will find it actually keeps them awake, rather than helping you go to sleep (due to the caffeine content in the chocolate, and sugar in the Milo). Instead, I suggest you give your child a hot chocolate or Milo in the morning as part of their breakfast, as it will give them some energy, help wake them up, and is a pleasant reinforcement for when they have had a good night's sleep.

Routine
This is such a simple concept and in fact so simple that many parents just ignore it because they can't see why it is so important, and sometimes because it actually impacts on them as well. Yet once a bedtime routine is established it makes things a lot less stressful and easier for everyone.

When I talk about routine, I mean the same things happening at the same time every night, and morning. However, this does not mean 'to the minute' or 'exactly like this', but it does mean within 15 minutes of the set time and pretty much the same thing. Let me explain this by giving some examples:

Johnny gets into his PJ's between 7.30pm and 7.45pm each night, the rule being he must have them on by 7.45pm at the latest. Between 7.45pm and 8pm, he needs to brush his teeth, go to the toilet and get into bed ready for his bedtime story. His Mum or Dad then go to Johnny at 8pm, read him his story for around 10 – 15 minutes, say goodnight to him, and turn off his bedroom light. The next morning at 7.15am Johnny's Mum or Dad open his curtains, turn his light on and say "good morning Johnny" to make sure he is awake. They go back at 7.30am, where if he hasn't got himself out of bed, they assist him with verbal prompts to get him up and start dressing for school. He must be dressed and be out of his room and having breakfast by 7.40am, and ready to leave for school, with his bag packed, by 8.10am.

Sarah, is now a young teenager (13), and so her bedtime routine isn't quite as strict as Johnny's is, but because sleep/bedtime has been a problem for her, her Caregivers have set up a specific routine. She can watch TV, or have time on the computer up until 9pm. By 9pm she must go to her room, where she can do what she wants, as long as her light is off by 9.30pm, and she is in bed. At 7am, her caregivers knock on her door, and give her a wake up "good morning, time to get up". Sarah knows she must be up, dressed, and having her breakfast by 7.20am, or her caregivers knock on her door again and insist she gets up then, and gets to the breakfast table.

Of course each child and household will differ slightly, but the principles shown in the examples are that a pattern is formed of the tasks and/or times that certain parts of the bedtime process happen, and these are kept to as close as possible. This in turn means that those tasks/times will act as cues to the child in time, and they in themselves will signal the child that it is time to get ready for bed, which in turn means its times to get to sleep.

One rule though that must be kept to is sticking to a set bedtime, or 15 minutes either side of it. If you allow your child to go to bed at any old time, say between 9pm and 10.30pm, they will choose the 10.30pm and even try and push the boundaries around that. In turn, they are not giving their body the opportunity to set a sleep pattern, and sleeping will remain a problem for them.

Returning

If your child gets back out of bed, and "wants to stay up", simply return them to their room, and to their bed. Say nothing to them except a quiet and calm "It's time for sleeping now". Older children, especially those 13 years old and older can be more difficult with this. Yes, I too have had the "I'm not going to bed, I'm a teenager now...." type of argument with my kids. To combat this, (and the first few nights may impact on you and others too), you need to follow the advice below as it is one of the most effective strategies for this problem. If your teenager will not go to bed, or returns from bed when they are supposed to be there sleeping, give them the verbal prompt of "You need to be in bed asleep now, please go back to your room". Don't get into any argument or discussion, just keep to this prompt. Give them the prompt twice, a minute or two between each if they still argue. If they still will not go back to bed, turn off the TV, computer, and any other entertainment type device, and turn all lights off. If they insist on turning these things back on, then you are facing a "Teenage Compliance Issue" and you need to read the specific chapter in this book - "Behaviour Skills for Parents, Teachers and Support People – 2nd Edition" about dealing with this. If they don't try and turn things back on, then just ignore them, go to your room, and eventually they will make their way to bed. You may need to repeat this for a few nights, but eventually most teenagers will understand that they are simply wasting their time coming out of their room, because everything just gets turned off if they do.

Praise

Most parents do not let their children know they are pleased that they have gone to bed on time, and stayed in bed all night. It seems to be a 'taken for granted' aspect of a child's life. As you would have learnt from the book "Behaviour Skills for Parents and Support People", the likelihood of a behaviour being repeated in the future, is determined by what happens immediately after the behaviour. Of course sleep is a necessary biological function, and so is not really governed by reinforcement.

However, we all quickly learn that if we don't get enough sleep the night before, we feel tired and grumpy the next day, and when we get a great night's sleep we (usually) feel refreshed and less stressed the next day. So, if you add to this your verbal praise of "I'm so happy with you Johnny, you went to bed on time, and stayed in bed all night, good boy!" it will definitely help to encourage your child to get to bed on time, and stay in bed again the following night.

You should also praise your child for each step of the routine they follow, especially in its early stages when you are establishing the routine. For example "Good girl, you had your teeth brushed by 7.30, well done!" Many Parents and Caregivers I have worked with have found the use of a reward chart system very helpful in establishing sleeping routines, and 'staying in bed all night' behaviour. Read the chapter on 'Use of the Dior Method Reward Cards System' in the book "Behaviour Skills for Parents and Support People" for information on how to utilise a chart like this if you feel your child may need that extra bit of encouragement.

The Extras

There are some extra things that will be helpful with specific sleep related problems. These are listed below, under the headers of the sleep problem they specifically help to address.

Not wanting to go to bed/sleep

The Countdown: Let your child know, when it is 30 minutes before bedtime, 20 minutes before, 10 minutes, 5 minutes, and 1 minute before. This helps them start winding down, and becomes another cue for them to be prepared for bed and sleeping. You need to be firm around this though, and when that final minute is up, ensure they do go off to bed, or start the bedtime routine (change into PJs, brush teeth – or whatever the routine is). If you let them have "just one more minute" they will soon start doing this every time, and you will find the 30 minute countdown turns more into the 45 minute countdown, meaning 15 minutes past their bedtime.

Wanting to sleep elsewhere other than in their own bed

Firstly you need patience and perseverance. Trying to establish exactly why your child doesn't like their bed or bedroom would be helpful so you address the cause. It may be they are scared of the dark, noises outside, or simply likes the company and warmth of being in Mum and/or Dad's bed.

Reassurance each night at bedtime, while also not specifically mentioning their fears, will help if it is about their fear of the dark or outside noises, 'monster under the bed' etc. For example if they tell you they are scared of their cupboard "There is someone in it, who might get me when

I'm asleep.", when you put them to bed each night, go into the cupboard to get something, or put something away. Have them with you when you do this. Make it an extended task of say 2 or 3 minutes, so they can clearly see no person or 'thing' is in there. You don't need to actually state that, as this just puts focus back on what they are fearing and won't help the situation. If it is a fear of the dark, a night light, or the light in the hallway being left on may be a simple solution. However, in some cases, it will take a little more to get your child back to sleeping in their own bed.

Those children who are really resisting staying in their bed, or getting in their bed to start with, will need some extra reassurance and a strategy that is not aversive yet will have success. Beware that some helpful souls like 'Super Nanny' use quite aversive methods to get children to sleep in their own beds, and I do not agree with or advise you use these. These have included the desperate parent clinging to the door handle on the other side of the bedroom door, sometimes for 30 minutes or more, while an extremely distressed and frightened child on the other side screams and cries. Eventually, this may work in that the child will give up trying to leave their room at night, but the fear and resentment you instil in the child at the same time, is hardly worth the result, especially when there are other much less aversive ways to deal with the problem.

So, here is what you will need to do. Put a chair in your child's room, about a metre from their bed, but where they can still see you. Before bedtime that first night, explain that you are going to be putting them in their own bed tonight, but you are going to stay in their room with them. You may need to fight quite a strong will, in that they have been allowed to sleep in your bed before, so why this change.

You need to be firm, and give no other option. Once they are in bed (follow the other recommendations outlined in the 'Dior Method' at the start of the chapter to get them there to start with) sit down in the chair, and rest. Do not talk with them, or make direct eye contact after the first couple of minutes. This is where the perseverance and patience comes in. You will need to stay in that chair until they are fast asleep. This may take 30 minutes, it may take a couple of hours or so! The next night same thing again, but have the chair about another 30 cms away from their bed. Repeat this night after night, until eventually your chair is out of the doorway, in which case you stand in the doorway instead. Then the next night, you stand just out of sight, but reassure them you are still there by making some noise, like cleaning or tidying. Do not respond to them, if they call your name, but if they start getting too upset, just walk past the doorway, so they see you are still there.

How Much Sleep Do We Really Need?

AGE	SLEEP NEEDED each night
Newborns (1 - 2 months)	10.5 – 18 hours
Infants (3 - 11 months)	9 - 12 hours during the night and 30 minute to two hour naps one to four times each day
Toddlers (1-3 years)	12 - 14 hours
Preschoolers (3 - 5 years)	11 - 13 hours
School-aged Children (5 - 12 years)	10 - 11 hours
Teens (13 – 17 years)	8.5 – 9.25 hours
Adults (18 years +)	7 – 9 hours

Source: 'Sleep Foundation'

Though the above table is a good guide for average amounts of sleep required according to the person's age, each individual differs. Some people may need more sleep, some may need less. A fairly good rule of thumb is, if your child appears to be sleepy during the day, or is always wanting to take naps (or simply falling asleep while playing) they probably need more sleep at night time.

> If you are concerned about how tired your child appears to be, even when they seem to be getting a reasonable night's sleep, you should consult your GP and have them checked for any possible medical condition that may be leading to their tiredness.

Frequent Criers

Firstly we need to remember the basics that this book tries to ensure everyone understands. The main basic of behaviour being that 'every behaviour has a function for the person emitting that behaviour'. In this case, there IS a reason why your child cries almost every time you put them to bed, and may cry for a long period of time. Finding what the function is, is very important in knowing what the right approach to take is in reducing or stopping that crying from happening each night.

Frightened?

As already discussed, many children cry at night when put to bed, because they are frightened of the dark. Crying itself may have originally started because it was their way of expressing their fear, but then it has subsequently become reinforced by the fact that Mum, Dad, or their caregiver comes to them because they are crying, and of course the dark isn't so frightening if someone else is there with you. The child has now learnt that getting someone else there is achieved by crying.

What to do
Being frightened of the dark is of course a phobia, if that is the true reason behind the crying. There is a chapter in the book 'Behaviour Skills for Parents and Support People' that specifically addresses ways of helping reduce or eliminate phobias, so have a read of that for some advice if you are really struggling after trying these suggestions. Also, try the good old 'night light', as it may be all that is required.

Firstly, you need to talk to your child in a way so they are reassured that they are safe in their room. You don't need to talk about 'the dark' specifically, more so about how nice and comfy their room is, and how close they are to the other bedrooms or other people in the house when they go to bed.

Also ensure you have a bedtime routine in place that involves spending some time in their room when they first go to bed, maybe reading a story, **then also for a few minutes in their room after the light is turned off**. When the light is turned off, talk about what it is they are doing the next day, focus on the positives "What are you looking forward to most?", and "What is something fun we can do when we both get home tomorrow?". This way you are helping them think about nice things while being in the dark, and so helping to refocus them off their fear while they think of other things, as well as have them feeling happy and settled while being in the dark.

Once you leave the room, if they start to cry, don't go back in immediately but wait a minute or two (as long as they are not getting hysterically upset, where they will need a lot of comforting to settle them down). When you do go back in, only go just inside the door, say "It's ok" wait a minute at most, then leave. Repeat this as many times as you need for the first few nights, though increasing the delay slightly each time. This way they are getting used to being in the dark, and everything still being ok – as you eventually do come.

You should find that if following this consistently, after one to two weeks, the problem should cease; If it doesn't, look at increasing the light available, then slowly decreasing the amount of light over the period of one to two weeks. For example: a lamp on a dimmer switch, or a light in the hall being on, then a bathroom light. Bering frightened of the dark can be a long term issue for many, with some people carrying it into adulthood. But with consistency, and always remaining calm and patient, you should make progress using these strategies.

Frustrated / Annoyed?

Another fairly common reason is that your child may be frustrated or annoyed that they have had to go to bed, when they wanted to stay up and watch TV, play on the computer, or just be with everyone else who is still up and about and "having fun" (that may be their perception). So again, they may have first cried because it was their way of expressing their annoyance, but this was then reinforced by parents or others who let them come back out and join the family, sometimes just because it was easier than having to listen to them cry! The child has now learned that if they cry long or loud enough, eventually someone will give in and let them come back out of their bedroom.

What to do

Firstly, routine is very important here. Your child really needs to know exactly when their bedtime is, and that it is stuck to as close as possible, one way or another. If they just go to bed when the parent or caregiver decides it is their time to go to bed, they will of course get frustrated and upset, where as if it is the bedtime they always go at, they will be more accepting of this.

Having what I call a 'countdown warning' is also helpful with this behaviour. Have a ten minute, five minute, and a one minute verbal prompt. "Ok James, ten more minutes until your bedtime", and then the same approach for the next two prompts. If you find your child still protests even with the prompts, try adding a twenty minute prompt as well.

"What do I get out of it?" That is the question that believe it or not, we all ask ourselves with almost everything we do. You may not be consciously aware of it, but you will want to be getting something from each and every behaviour you emit. It is the same with a child at bedtime, others are staying up to watch TV, so what do I get out of going to bed now? Of course we aren't going to promise this, that, and the other, just to get them to go to bed on time each and every night without crying.

But what we can do is make going to bed, and staying in bed quietly a much more pleasant experience, so it is not something to dread.

For example, have a bedtime story, or special five minutes with Mum, Dad or other family member to talk about what they are going to do tomorrow. This leads you into talking about how great it is to get some sleep so they have energy for tomorrow's activity, and the sooner they get to sleep the sooner tomorrow will be there. If their next day doesn't have anything overly exciting to look forward to, introduce a special activity for either the morning or after school. This may be playing a game with you, helping cook a special breakfast, or other preferred activity.

Lastly, ensure others respect the fact that your child has just gone to bed. Turn the TV down as low as possible, radios and computers turned down, and ensure people are not talking loudly or playing outside or near the child's bedroom. If you still really struggle, you can set up a system where if they stay in bed and are quiet, you will come and see them every ten minutes. If you do this, make it only a very brief visit, where you step in to their room, say "Good girl/boy, well done for being nice and quiet" then step back out. Over the next few days, extend the ten minute checks to fifteen minutes, then twenty, and so on. Eventually you should see your child just falling asleep naturally, and - all going to plan, quietly!

Just Not Comfortable?
Though this would be a much rarer reason for a child to cry every night when going to bed, it can happen. It may be that the child dislikes their bed or bedclothes. Maybe their bedroom is too hot,

cold, damp, or just plain messy! If they are not sure how to communicate that they are not comfortable in their bed or bedroom, crying may be how they try and let you know. Yes, again, this behaviour may be reinforced if parents or caregivers give in and let them sleep somewhere else. Of course, the actual problem itself does need to be addressed to reduce or stop the behaviour, and to be fair on the child of course.

What to do
A fairly simple checklist should get things right with this issue. Go through the following with your child, and only tick off each one when you and your child agree with it.

- Is their bed comfortable, not too hard or too soft?
- Does their bed always have nice clean bed sheets and blanket/duvet?
- Is their bedroom warm, but not too warm?
- Is there enough light, or too much light?
- Do they feel safe in their bedroom; do the windows close properly, securely?
- Is their pillow comfortable, enough or not enough pillows?
- Do they 'like' their bedroom? Do they want to put some pictures on the walls, or change their curtains or bed sheets/duvet? Do they want/need some soft toys to make them feel more comfortable and secure?
- Is anyone bothering them at night time?
- Is their bedroom kept clean and tidy?

Preventing the Pain
Successful Parenting = Successful Children

"Why do they do these things, and make my life a pain?", that is the question that many parents ask themselves as they watch their children fighting or making a huge mess, or showing other unwanted behaviour. The answer, or at least a very big part of it is – You need to start early with teaching appropriate behaviour to your child, if you want to prevent many years (or many more years) of potential headaches.

No matter whether your child is neuro-typical (without a diagnosed disability) or has autism, intellectual disability or other disability, the earlier you start teaching them the better.

Think of your young child's brain being like a hard drive on a computer, an almost blank hard drive. It is waiting for the programs and data to be entered into it telling it how to do things. The programs, being the general framework of how we do things – speaking to people respectfully, politely, or otherwise! How we handle dangerous equipment, even things as basic as the oven or hot kettle. The data is the finer details that fill the gaps, such as having explained why we don't touch the hot oven, and why we have to be careful how we pour out the boiling water. Those who enter this information are all those people the child comes across each day particularly in the years up to around eight years of age.

Parents, whether they are the biological parents, adoptive parents, foster parents or guardians who have been given the wonderful yet challenging opportunity to raise a child, are the key people who will shape that child. Again, just as with a computer, how the person enters the information, as well as the quality and commitment of their efforts, will determine how well that child in turn uses that information. Of course if the 'data' is corrupt, that is – the fine details were missing or simply incorrect, that child may struggle in many parts of its life.

So the big question is "how do we do this right then?" The answer to this question will of course depend on our own experiences before we became a parent. How many times have you seen or heard on the news media, stories about parents or caregivers who have battered or even murdered their child, and they go on to describe how they too were the victims of domestic violence or a severely deprived childhood? It is difficult to teach something that we didn't necessarily experience ourselves as children. Difficult – but not impossible!

As Parents, we need to 'get over' what we may have missed out on as children, just because we may not have had a lot of time spent with us from our Parents, is no excuse to then go on and spend little time with our children. The saying 'learn from your mistakes' is very apt here, and we can take from what may have even been a terrible childhood, a lesson on how to be a great Parent, because we know that what we experienced can not be repeated to our own children. We need to look at the basics of parenting, and ensure we do these things. Below are some very simple, very basic, minimum standards that we should ensure we do with our children each and every day.

- ✓ **One on one time, for at least twenty minutes every day:** This means just you, and your child, talking about the day. What did they do, what did you do, or even just reading a book together or drawing some pictures. If you have more than one child, then give each of them some one on one time, as well as at least a few minutes with everyone together. This is a general guideline for children from around eight years of age to 13 years of age. Each year younger than eight, add another ten minutes per year (so, a seven year old would get 30 minutes, and a five year old 40 minutes - at least), children over 13 should still get at least ten minutes one to one each day. For toddlers (1 to 3 years old) you should be having regular one-to-one times with them every day, I suggest at least one 10 minute period every waking hour where possible. Of course giving your child this one on one time, doesn't mean you ignore them the rest of the day! No, not at all, it just means that you are ensuring you give them that special few minutes to talk, or just be together, with no distractions (meaning NO TV on, and NO Video Games during this time). Also remember I emphasise this is a *minimum* amount of time for one to one, *not a maximum!*

- ✓ **Behavioural Correction:** There is a difference between 'nagging' and what I term 'behavioural correction'. I suggest you use behavioural correction whenever it is required, without getting to the stage where you won't let your child, be a child. For example, if you see your child eat a snack, then simply throw the rubbish on the ground, don't just say "Hey, pick that up now, what is wrong with you?", that is what I would term nagging. Instead correct the behaviour, and use the opportunity to teach your child what is right, and why, and increase the chances that next time they will show the appropriate behaviour. *"George, what should you do when you open a snack bar? Yes that's right, you need to put the rubbish straight into the bin, so let's go do that right now. Do you see lots of rubbish on the street when you walk to school? Yes? That is what happens if people don't put their rubbish in the bin. Great job, it is so good to see you put your wrapper into the bin, well done."* Yes, this will take a minute of your time, and no – I don't expect you to give mini lectures every time your child does something wrong, but when you get a chance like in this example, to give a 'behavioural correction', then take it! Often working on getting these little things right, will have impacts on the bigger stuff later in life, as it teaches discipline, and that there are some standards that society expects (or should expect) from each and every one of us.

- ✓ **Three Positive Things:** The last minimum thing we should do as parents each day, is make sure we say at least three positive things to each child. They don't all have to be at the same time, you might say one in the morning "You are always up out of bed early James, I am really happy you do that, thank you", one after they get home from school "You are out of your uniform straight after school just like you do every day. I am so lucky I have such a good girl who does that, thank you Mary.", and at bed time "You do a great job at brushing your teeth, well done!". Again, this is minimum that is good to set for yourself, always try and take a positive approach to parenting, as it ends up being a lot less stressful for everyone.

The above very basic principles are so easy to do, yet so many parents do none of them. Instead they seem to spend all their time telling their child off "Don't do that, why did you do that, tidy that up, I hate having kids!". When a child hears these negative comments over and over, the Parents' comments become a bit like static on a radio, annoying, meaningless, and nothing to take any real notice of. Also, of course, we as parents do not like having to constantly tell our child off for something they have done wrong, wouldn't it be better and easier to give more positive comments than negative comments?

The rest of this chapter concentrates on exactly how we can change from our current negative parenting ways, or for new parents how you can become a great positive parent, and we can all 'prevent the pain'!

Changing Our Own Behaviour: If we want to change our children's' behaviour, using a positive approach, we first need to change our own behaviour. To do this, you need to look at any 'bad habits' you may currently have. For example, every time you get annoyed, do you raise your voice to shouting level? Do you ever threaten or swear at others around your children? Do you always put your cups and plates away properly after you have used them, put your dirty laundry into the basket, keep your room tidy, etc?

Of course, none of us are angels, and many of us are guilty of one or more of the behaviours just mentioned. We can't expect to change our behaviour to the level of 'perfect', however at the same time, we can't expect our children to learn appropriate behaviour if what they see from us is not appropriate. So what we can do is start making a change to get these behaviours under control, and the fact that we are making progress with this is also a good lesson for our children. That lesson being, sometimes people get slack, they make mistakes, but the most important thing we can do is learn from those mistakes, and never give up trying to improve our own behaviour.

Also just being conscious of when children are around, and altering our behaviour and language accordingly is helpful. How many times have you seen documentaries, news items, or even real life examples of lesser quality parents swearing, putting down others or even using physical violence right in front of their own children? When you have seen this, have you thought "Wow, what chance do those kids stand for growing up to be decent citizens?" If this thought hasn't crossed your mind, to be blunt – it should have! We wouldn't hesitate to put a teacher down if she or he spoke in front of a classroom full of kids like that, but somehow some of us feel it's ok as Parents to talk or behave in that manner in front of our own children.

To make changing our own behaviour easier, we need to know exactly what we do at the moment that may not be helpful in shaping our children for their future lives. To do this, it is beneficial to write a list titled '**My Bad Habits**'. This list will just be for you, so be totally and ruthlessly honest.

For some it may a look a little like this:

My Bad Habits

- Swearing
- Shouting
- Not making my bed in the morning
- Eating way to many takeaways
- Leaving dirty dishes on the table
- Not spending any quality time with the kids

Of course not everyone will have these things on their lists, some may have completely different habits, less bad habits, or more bad habits. Either way, spending a few minutes now to write down a list will be helpful in reducing or even stopping these habits.

What will you replace them with? If it is a behaviour, or 'habit', that you want to reduce or stop, like swearing, you need to think about what you are going to replace it with. Just like you will learn when you read the rest of this book, if you are to stop or reduce an unwanted behaviour in your child, you need to teach them something else they CAN do instead of emitting that behaviour. This same rule applies to you to. For example, if it is swearing you want to reduce, give yourself an alternative word or phrase you can use instead when you are angry or annoyed. For example "Darn it" or "Oh man!". These are a lot more acceptable to use around your children, and they too may learn to use them instead of other less desirable words!

If it is a behaviour that you need to introduce, such as remembering to put your dirty dishes straight into the dishwasher or sink, you need to remember a couple of things. One, what will you use to help you to remember to do this? A sign in the kitchen, asking your kids to remind you, or telling yourself each morning and each night before bed for a couple of weeks "From now on the dishes go in the sink"? Secondly, what will you reinforce (reward) your new behaviour with? A treat at the end of a week remembering it (a chocolate bar or a glass of wine maybe?), or a sleep in on Sunday morning? These principles are the secret in achieving behaviour change for yourself, so don't ignore the advice and face possible failure!

What does it mean to be a Parent?
Many of us enter Parenthood, without really giving this question much, if any, real thought. Some times it is a surprise (or even a shock!) to find out you are about to become a first time parent, or you

are about to have another child. Even for those who have planned the pregnancy, and planned on being a parent, when the baby is actually born and you change from a "couple, no children" to a "Couple with one of more children" it can be a shock at how much life changes.

There are those people who simply carry on as they did before they had a child, and try and convince others, as well as themselves, that nothing has changed, I still party, socialise, etc. I believe that it is this category of people who may in fact end up having the biggest parenting problems later on, and subsequently have children with either severe behavioural, emotional, or social difficulties. These parents come from all parts of society, low, middle and high income brackets, possibly more common in the low and high income brackets.

If you honestly believe you can be an effective and successful parent while keeping almost exactly the same lifestyle you had before children, then you are setting yourself and your child/children up for disappointment, if not disaster.

So, what is the main difference between having no children, and having one or more children of your own? In other words, what does it mean to be a parent? I believe this can be summed up in two main categories.

- **Commitment:** You need to commit time, energy, love, resources and thought. You must spend time with your child at home, out in society, and to some degree at kindergarten and then at school.

The amount of quality time you spend with your child, will determine the strength of the relationship you have with them through the rest of their life, and the amount of knowledge they pick up from you. As for 'thought', I include this as I believe you need to continually think through how best to meet your child's needs. Think about how you approach problems that may arise for them, and think about what you are doing that will enable them to get through life successfully. Love does come naturally, but you need to commit to it's growth and development between you and your child, or it may gradually fade to a bare existence that has no value to you or your child any more. Energy is what will be drained from you every day, if you don't commit to getting enough sleep, eating right, and exercising. This commitment is life long, and so planning on getting 'your own life back' when your child turns 18, isn't a plan you should be making. Though of course when they reach the age of 18, they are nearing adulthood – this doesn't mean their need for your love, energy, and support will simply disappear.

- **Acceptance of Ownership:** I am sure many will argue with the term 'ownership' in regards to one's own children, but I believe this may be why we see so much child neglect, abuse, and teenage anti-social behaviour. Parenting a child means taking ownership of them, their behaviour and the consequences of their behaviour. The attitude of "It's not my fault they are a bad kid, and they tag, steal, assault, lie, cheat...." is completely incorrect. **IT IS YOUR FAULT!** Take ownership of your child, know where they are, what they doing, who they are with, what school work they have, how successful they are in relation to grades at school, and so on. If you don't take ownership, who will? Gangs? Homeless people? The local paedophile? Your child is a product of you and your partner, and as such you are 100% responsible for them until the age they start taking successfully taking responsibility for their own behaviour. I believe the earliest age for this is 21, and for many it may be even older, or possibly almost lifelong. If you are not willing to accept this, then don't have children.

Managing Teenage behaviour

Becoming a teenager is possibly one of the most important transitions we make in life. It is the 'bridge' between being a child, and becoming what society terms 'an adult'. In modern times, maybe the last fifteen years or so, teenage years seem to begin even before the child reaches their teenage years. Some 12 year olds, and even 11 year olds now engage in behaviours that once were the regime of 14 and 15 year olds. Where in turn, some 13 and 14 year olds now engage in behaviours that were once mainly seen only in 18 and 19 year olds. These behaviours may include sexual relationships (or seemingly more common – sex without the relationship), over indulging in alcohol, illicit drug use, and so on.

With these changes in society, it is no wonder that many parents either just give up, and let their 12 year olds, and older, just run wild, or they lose their patience, and maybe discipline them in ways that are both harmful and even illegal in some cases. It is with this in mind that I decided to write this, all be it short, chapter to hopefully assist parents in how to get their teenage children back on track, or at least aimed in the right direction. It isn't easy, and just parents by themselves, without the support of other family members and hopefully the school, may still struggle to right the behaviours they are now experiencing the effects of. However, being armed with some ideas and strategies is better than struggling along with seemingly no hope of a brighter future for your teenage children, or by default – yourself.

In a different style from the rest of this book, I have set out some strategies alongside the more common issues parents now face. I hope this will be an easier option for you, in your obviously already hectic and stressful life managing your teenage child.

Teenage Behaviour Problem	Recommended Approach / Strategy
Swearing at, and/or talking back to Parents rudel,y and defiance.	Firstly, learn to stay in control of your behaviour and the language you are using. If you raise your voice, or swear back, you are simply feeding into what they are looking for – a 'power struggle', or argument, that they plan on winning one way or another. If your teenager has 'talked back' (ie. "Why don't you put the dishes away", or "I'll clean my room when I want to"), don't answer back straight away. Wait a minute or so, then calmly but firmly give the request again. If they still reply with a similar refusal or rude comment, wait another 20 seconds or so before making any comment; then again give the request, explaining the positive consequence first, and then the negative consequence.

	EG: *"David, you need to clean your room now. Pickup up all the rubbish and place it in the bin, and put your dirty clothes in the laundry. If you do this now, we will have time to talk about that DVD you want to buy, if you don't do this now, I won't have time to talk to you about the DVD until tomorrow"* Remember, we are not issuing a threat, or a punishment here, but more-so a natural consequence, good (positive) and bad (negative). If you still have no success, simply repeat the process from step one. You need to show you can stay calm, but still insist on them completing the task – you will get your way, and they won't get theirs – at least not until they have done what you requested first.
Lieing	If you know it's a lie that you are being told, don't get angry, instead simply point out that you know they are not being truthful, and if they won't tell you the truth, then you won't discuss the issue with them any more. But – because this doesn't really solve the issue, and your teenager may believe they have

	found a way of avoiding telling the truth, this isn't the end of the strategy. Though you do tell them you won't discuss the issue any more, you instead direct them to write down what the 'real story' is. Often teenagers, children, and sometimes adults find it hard to admit face to face to something they have done wrong, and so lie instead. However, many will find it easier to write down their admission of what really happened and hand this to the person concerned. If they refuse to write down what the 'real story' is, tell them (only when you are calm) that you are "disappointed in them". This is often more effective than telling them you are angry, or displaying anger. This will hopefully see them think about what has happened, and eventually they will come around to telling you the truth, or at least think more carefully next time about being truthful with you.
Associating with a 'bad crowd'	Some teenagers seem to be magnets to trouble makers. That is, the friends they have are almost always 'bad', in that they are in trouble with teachers, police, or just generally not nice kids.

Firstly we need to ask ourselves 'Is my teenager in fact the 'bad one'?' Whether they are or not, it is usually when there is a group or audience that your child will behave in an unacceptable way. This is what is often termed 'peer pressure', or being encouraged by others to do what they would not usually do.

The strategy for dealing with this is very simple, yet very hard to implement without 100% commitment and consistency from you. If you don't have this, then you might as well give up – and of course if you give up, you are possibly resigning to the fact your child will get themselves deeper and deeper into trouble as they get older.

So number one – DON'T GIVE UP! That is your son, your daughter – you brought them into this World, and I am sure that, even if deep down, you want them to be as successful as you are, if not more successful. Don't let a few months, maybe a couple of years, hard work parenting put you off helping your teenager get back on the right track.

Strategy steps:

1) DON'T GIVE UP!

2) Do some research. Find out where they really go, who they are really hanging around with, and the most common days and times this happens. We will call these the 'trouble times'.

3) Start filling in your teenagers 'trouble times' with fun activities with you. When I say fun, I mean what they would call fun, not what you would call fun. Make an agreement with them at least the day before, or even a couple of days before that you will do this fun activity at *this time, on this day.* If they say that is when they will be with their mates, tell them they will need to make another time to meet them, because this is the only time you can do that activity. You will need to be insistent and firm about this, but don't go over the top and scare

them off. If it is an activity attractive enough to them, they probably won't mind missing seeing their friends that day.

4) Break the habit. By filling in the 'trouble times' with fun activities, or 'must do' events on a regular basis for three or four weeks, you will be breaking their old habit of hanging around the trouble makers, and forming a new habit of doing worthwhile activities.

5) Praise, praise and more praise. Whenever they have chosen a different activity from hanging around with trouble makers, tell them how pleased and proud you are at seeing them do – what it is they are doing. However, DON'T use the term 'trouble makers' or refer to their friends in a bad light at all, as this may just encourage them to be rebellious and go with them just to spite you.

	6) Set boundaries. If they are going out somewhere, DO get them to agree on a time to be back home. Set some natural consequences around this. Always give the positive consequence first. EG. *"If you are back on time, we will have time for a nice hot chocolate, and a talk about what to do in the holidays. If you aren't back at the time, that you agreed on, then there will be no time for a hot chocolate, and I will have to decide on what we will do in the holidays by myself."*
The almost compulsory Messy Room	Firstly, don't stress too much. Believe it or not, many teenagers lives are more stressful than yours, or at the very least, your teenager believes their life is more stressful than yours. They have exams, difficult relationships with friends, bullies, temptations of alcohol, drugs, sex, and rebellion. Their minds on some days are just completely muddled. These muddled minds often mean messy disorganised rooms. In fact, I think Parents should be a little more concerned if their

> teenager's room was always perfectly clean and tidy!
>
> If their room is getting beyond just messy, and starting to resemble the local Zoo dung collection area, there are ways of getting it back to some sort of order.
>
> Set small goals for your teenager to achieve each couple of days. The first might be to bring their dirty washing to the laundry by tomorrow night at 7pm. Be specific about the timing, and give them a friendly reminder a couple of hours before the time, and again 30 minutes before the time. Praise them when they have done it. *"Excellent, great to see you deal with that washing, thank you."*

Respect your Teenagers

Though you need to be firm with teenagers to successfully manage their sometimes chaotic behaviour, and you need to have strict and clear boundaries in place, this doesn't mean you shouldn't respect them.

In this context, I am referring to respecting them as being young adults – if only in their point of view and in their changing body. They are facing a very difficult and challenging life transition, and if they feel their parents do not have any respect for them, they are likely to rebel and/or become depressed.

Having respect for your teenagers includes:
- Always listening to what they have to say, whether you agree with it or not.
- Give some thought to their point of view, and try and give a reply that assures them you have thought about what they have said – and this is your decision (be it favourable to them or not)
- Sometimes letting them get their own way, but making sure they know you are LETTING them get their own way – not that they are doing what they want to do because they say so. In other words, let them discover (if safe to do so) for themselves that life is about trial and error sometimes.
- Accepting that they now have some feelings that you may not be entirely comfortable with ("My baby is no longer a baby!"). That is, girls will like boys more than just being friends, and vice versa. Or of course for some – they may like their own gender, and this you will need to accept whether you are comfortable with it or not.

Lastly, enjoy your teenagers. You may be saying, or possibly shouting "HOW, when they are so difficult?" Well – you just need to accept that they are now becoming what you once became and still are – an adult. It is challenging, stressful, yet inevitable – so you might as well go with it, and try and enjoy the journey with your teenager. Good luck!

IN SUMMARY OF BEHAVIOUR SKILLS

Knowledge and patience are possibly the two keys to making positive changes to a person's unwanted behaviours. Having the knowledge that this book has hopefully taught you, and increasing your patience in working through the strategies that either you or someone else constructs, should in most cases see a reduction or cessation to the behaviours of concern.

Knowing the antecedents, understanding the exact behaviour emitted, and looking at the responses or reinforcers to that behaviour, have all been highlighted numerous times throughout the text. This is for good reason, as they are the basics of behaviour itself. Some investigation is often required to work out what the antecedents are, and if there are certain events that take place each time before an incident occurs. Observing the person in the environment where most incidents occur, and discussing the incidents with the people who most often support the person concerned, will allow you to understand exactly what occurs when the unwanted behaviour occurs.

For the Parents who have purchased this book to aid them in managing and modifying a child's behaviour, I ask that you take a step back from what you experience with the challenges your child presents. Take an analytical approach, because most Parents (quite naturally) are often bound by their emotional connection not only to their child, but from the effects of the unwanted behaviour on them and the rest of the family. In other words, they sometimes look only for a solution, not a cause. Taking an analytical approach, as this book has taught you, will allow you to consider all factors of the challenging issues. You will look at what your responses are, and whether they could be reinforcing the behaviour. You will look at environmental causes, so looking at what happens around your child that may be triggering certain behaviours. Of course you will also be looking for the function of the behaviour, what exactly does your child get from emitting that behaviour? Once you have armed yourself with this knowledge, as well as ruling out any possible medical reasons, you can start working on a plan to get the behaviour modified.

Disability Organisations can improve immensely in how they manage people with unwanted behaviour. There is no excuse for having poorly trained staff or worse still staff with no training in behaviour management at all. The majority of Disability Organisations in New Zealand are left wanting when it comes to quality of support. The family members of the people you support, as well as the people supported, expect and deserve only the highest level of support, and that is exactly what they should receive. This book is vital in, at the very least, grounding support staff in the basics of behaviour. Online Courses are also offered by the organisation BehaviourSkills, and organisations should take advantage of these as part of their staff's core training.

Lastly, I would like to leave you with the following thoughts:

When every purposeful movement we make is termed behaviour, and behaviour is what affects every one of us 24 hours a day, seven days a week, we should at least have an understanding of it and learn as much as we can about it. Share your new knowledge of behaviour, and use it to improve the lives of those you support, because there is no reason people must live their lives around another person's unwanted behaviour.

Author - Trevor Lewis

Trevor Lewis can be contacted via email at www.behaviourskills.com

INDEX

A

ABC
  Recording Chart, **- 44 -**
Anger Management
  Helpful Hints, - 248 -
  Rules for Anger, - 243 -
  Stop, - 236 -
  Strategy Form, - 250 -
  Walk Away, - 238 -
ANGER MANAGEMENT, - 228 -
Anxiety, - 137 -
Applied Behaviour Analysis, - 15 -
Autism, - 151 -
  Being In an Alien World, - 151 -
  Concrete Thinking, - 154 -
  Early Intervention and Social Skills, - 156 -
  Sensory Sensitivity, - 160 -
  Step - By - Step, - 154 -
  Visual Prompts, - 155 -
  What Is It, - 151 -

B

Baseline, - 35 -
Behaviour
  Alternative, **- 101 -**, **- 103 -**
  Considerations of, **- 54 -**
  defining, - 21 -
  definition of, - 10 -
  first considerations, **- 18 -**
  Functions Of, - 36 -
  Incompatible, **- 101 -**, **- 105 -**
  Observing, **- 45 -**
  science of, - 14 -
  Teaching Wanted, **- 107 -**
Behaviour Chains
  Backward Chaining, - 34 -
  Definition, - 32 -
  Forward Chaining, - 34 -
Behavioural Momentum, - 126 -
Behavioural Terms, - 27 -

C

Chaining, - 107 -
  Backward, **- 115 -**
  Forward, **- 114 -**
Compliance Issues, - 183 -
Consistency, - 71 -
  Working as a Team, **- 57 -**
Crisis Prevention
  Team Work and Consistency, - 141 -
Cultural and Religious Beliefs. *See* ulture and Religious Beliefs

D

Desensitisation, - 73 -

E

Early Warning Signs
  recognition, - 136 -
Extinction, - 67 -
  Dangers Of, - 102 -
  Placing Behaviour On, - 100 -

Risks, - 70 -
Use of, **- 102 -**
What is it, - 67 -
Eye Contact, - 156 -

F

Fetal Alcohol Spectrum Disorder (FASD), - 163 -

G

Generalisation
Prompts and Behaviour, - 124 -

H

How To Use This Book, - 7 -

I

Intellectual Disability, - 143 -

K

Keeping Safe, - 140 -

M

Make Up of Behaviour
Antecedents, - 21 -
behaviour, - 24 -
consequence, - 24 -
Modeling, - 55 -
Modeling and Prompting, - 119 -
Modeling Appropriate Behaviour, - 119 -

O

Observation
Incidental Recordings, - 45 -
Naturalistic, - 46 -

P

Picture Exchange System, - 148 -
Preventing A Crisis, - 136 -
Preventing the Pain
Pro-active Parenting, - 270 -
Privacy, - 60 -
Prompting, - 122 -
Psychological Safety, - 62 -
Punishment, - 30 -
Myths, **- 83 -**
What is it, **- 82 -**

R

Reinforcement
Appropriate Behaviour, - 56 -
maintenance, - 98 -
Positive, **- 79 -**
What is it, **- 79 -**
Reinforcers
Bridging, **- 88 -**
Fading of, **- 96 -**
Pairing of Primary and Secondary, - 88 -
Positive, Negative, - 29 -
Respect, - 55 -
Response Cost, - 128 -

S

Safety, - 59 -
From Allegations, - 65 -
Self Injurious Behaviour
and extinction, - 71 -
Children, - 189 -
Self Stimulation Behaviour.
See stereotypical behaviour

Sensory Sensitivity, - 187 -
Sleep Problems, - 251 -
SUMMARY, - 292 -

T

Target Behaviour, - 27 -
Task Analysis
   Definition, - 32 -
   Examples, **- 112 -**
Teenage behaviour, - 281 -
The Dior Method
   ABCR, **- 172 -**

Analysis of Your Childs
Behaviour, **- 171 -**
Behaviour Categories, **- 180 -**
Data Analysis, **- 175 -**
Your Response, **- 182 -**
TOILET TRAINING, - 190 -

U

Unwanted Behaviour
Reducing, **- 99 -**

BehaviourSkills.com is my website that is dedicated to upskilling people about behaviour, by way of offering my behaviour management resources.

www.behaviourskills.com
upskilling people about behaviour

Further copies of this book can be purchased
via
www.behaviourskills.com or www.lulu.com

All contents Copyright Trevor Lewis 2011
Dunedin, New Zealand

ISBN

www.ingramcontent.com/pod-product-compliance
Lightning Source LLC
LaVergne TN
LVHW051111080426
835510LV00018B/1996